Classical Liberalism in the Age of
Post-Communism

Classical Liberalism in the Age of Post-Communism

Norman Barry

Professor of Politics
University of Buckingham

The Shaftesbury Papers, 6
Series Editor: Charles K. Rowley

Edward Elgar
Cheltenham, UK • Brookfield, US

Published by
Edward Elgar Publishing Limited
Glensanda House
Montpellier Parade
Cheltenham
Glos GL50 1UA
UK

Edward Elgar Publishing Company
William Pratt House
9 Dewey Court
Northampton
Massachusetts 01060
US

This book has been printed on demand to keep the title in print.

British Library Cataloguing in Publication Data
Barry, Norman, 1944–
  Classical liberalism in the age of post-communism. – (The
  Shaftesbury Papers; 6)
  1. Liberalism   2. Post-communism   3. Classical school of
  economics
  I.Title   II. Series
  320.5'1

Library of Congress Cataloguing in Publication Data
Barry, Norman P.
  Classical liberalism in the age of post-communism / Norman Barry,
  — (The Shaftesbury papers; 6)
  1. Liberalism. 2. Liberalism—History. 3. Civil society.
  4. Post-communism. I. Title. II. Series.
  JC574.B37   1996
  320.5'12—dc20   95–40188
                                                          CIP

ISBN 978 1 85898 256 4

Contents

Preface

I am indebted to Charles Rowley, General Director of the Locke Institute, for first suggesting that I write this book. His help and encouragement have been invaluable. I learnt much from a Locke Institute colloquium on classical liberalism which was sponsored by the Liberty Fund and held at Boston in June 1993. I am grateful to all the participants at this event for providing a lively discussion of some of the ideas that are analysed in this book.

I am especially grateful to the directors of the Social Philosophy and Policy Center, Bowling Green State University, Ohio, for allowing me to use their offices over the Christmas of 1993. Fred Miller, Jeffrey Paul and Ellen Frankel Paul provided their usual congenial and intellectually stimulating environment.

At Buckingham, I have improved my knowledge of economics and the social sciences from long conversations with Martin Ricketts, Professor of Economic Organisation at the University. He is particularly adept at working through the connections between political economy and social philosophy.

Finally, I must express great thanks to my secretary, Mrs Anne Miller, for her excellent work in preparing the manuscript for publication.

1. Introduction

It is a curious irony that in the aftermath of the collapse of communism, and the intellectual disintegration of the edifice of Marxism, the doctrine of classical liberalism should be in the same precarious state as it has been throughout much of this century. Its appeal to the intellectual class is no greater now than it was in the heyday of collectivism and much of its theoretical armoury, most notably its exposition of the necessity of market relationships if any sort of efficiency is to be achieved, has been subtly appropriated by exponents of doctrines whose aims are very different. Apparently, the market can be harnessed to serve social agendas and political purposes some way removed from those of the founders of the doctrines of individualism, private property and limited government.

What has occurred in the West is the rise of what Anthony de Jasay (1991) has correctly called 'loose' liberalism. This has consisted of a series of depredations of original classical liberal doctrine, not only in terms of successive policies which are alien to the tradition, but also by the corruption of the *language* in which these departures from individualistic orthodoxy are expressed and justified. Thus, the demand for individual freedom, which was once thought to be indissolubly linked to economic liberty, the exercise of which is almost certain to produce some inequality, has now become a licence for the state to maximize a notion of *equal* liberties; constitutionalism, which hitherto had provided a theoretical barrier to state intervention, has become a threadbare protection, in America especially, against a state powered by the democratic will; individual rights, which historically functioned as indefeasible side-constraints on political action, boundaries that determined the space within which individuals could pursue their self-determined goals, have lately become welfare entitlements, the granting of which requires positive action by the state; and justice is no longer a concept that describes the procedural rules under which individuals may contract with some predictability but has now become annexed to various 'end-states' (particular distributions of income and wealth) which the state may legitimately impose on a nominally free order.

The *desiderata* of the new flexible liberalism all concern freedom itself and the role of the state has been recommended to extend beyond even the promotion of equal liberties to the maximization of freedom as 'autonomy' (Raz, 1986; Gray, 1992). This means not merely the absence of restraint, and the possibility of uncoerced action within a protected sphere, but the creation of economic conditions in which individual choice is apparently a *true* reflection of options (Raz, 1986, pp. 409–10). In other words, social circumstances may coerce just as much as identifiable individual agents and restrictive laws do and it is the duty of the state to remove these allegedly freedom-reducing conditions.

In this context, the current fashion in political theory for 'communitarianism' (MacIntyre, 1981; Sandel, 1982; Walzer, 1983) has a little more intellectual respectability, or at least honesty.[1] For the communitarians attack the doctrine of individualism head on, they do not distort the concepts and language in which it was originally formulated but explicitly reject them. Their strictures apply just as much to the liberal egalitarians, who have appropriated the word liberalism while discarding its defining features, as they do to classical liberals. Communitarianism is specifically addressed to that universalism which is a feature of much liberal philosophy.

The most significant feature of communitarianism's rejection of liberal individualism is its frontal assault on the doctrine of the 'self' that underlies it. To the extent that classical liberalism has traditionally been founded upon certain more or less permanent features of the human condition (e.g. scarcity, limited altruism and an all-pervading ignorance with which human action has to cope) its quasi-scientific implications are never limited by time and place but offer prescriptions of a more or less universal application. Again, the purely ethical claims that it makes derive from a moral ontology which relates to abstract persons rather than to members of identifiable groups, sociologically-understood communities or ethnic associations. The communitarian claim, however, is that 'the kind of society in which people live...affects their understandings both of themselves and how they should lead their lives' (Mulhall and Swift, 1992, pp. 13–14). This inevitably introduces a strain of relativism into normative argument which is alien to almost all forms of liberalism.

The various claims embodied in the above statement can be reduced to the proposition that the *abstract* individual (of either classical liberalism or liberal egalitarianism) is an inadequate focal point for the construction of a coherent social philosophy; our institutional arrangements and social policies cannot conceivably be understood as products of individual choice and that the individualistic programme cannot be simply exported to communities whose cultural traditions may be quite unreceptive to its apparent *asocial* foundations. Political and economic arrangements are received not chosen and it is our interpretation of them that must inform whatever judgements we might make about distributive criteria, the limits of the market or the permissible bounds of personal liberty. From this perspective the constitutional constructivism (and, ultimately, libertarian economics) of James Buchanan (Buchanan and Tullock, 1962; Buchanan, 1975) or the 'thought experiment' of Rawls (1971), which is designed to generate a rationally acceptable and socially just redistribution of resources, are equally condemnable.

The current difficulties of establishing liberal market orders in post-communist society may lend a superficial credence to this point of view; the impression is that the classical liberal order itself is rooted in particular historical circumstances which, by definition, do not always prevail and cannot be easily transported. However, if the communitarian claim is that liberal economics has historically neglected the institutional (legal and political) framework in which market transactions take place, it is simply false: the literature, from Adam Smith to Hayek and beyond, is replete with explanations of such necessary social structures, and accounts of their emergence. Only in the driest of technical, neo-classical economic theory is 'abstract' man completely abstract. The fact that this institutional framework can and does vary from society to society is not a surrender to relativism (which is a clear implication of communitarian theory) but merely a recognition of that diversity which is a feature of all social arrangements. Indeed, classical liberalism, which merely puts boundaries to coercive state action, encourages such diversity and is compatible with a variety of institutional arrangements as long as certain liberties are protected.

However, the fragility of classical liberal theory has not only been highlighted by liberal egalitarians and communitarians, it has also been a feature of the work of some of its leading exponents. I refer here specifically to the later ideas of F.A. Hayek (1979, 1988). Here that *critical* rationalism which gives classical liberalism its vitality, cutting edge and claim to a qualified universalism, has been almost completely jettisoned in favour of a curious, neo-Darwinistic form of social evolutionism. Although this idea was nascent in Hayek's earlier writings outside economics, the anti-rationalist tenor of those works (Hayek, 1960) was primarily directed at constructivistic and socialistic theories that dispensed with spontaneous market processes in favour of the directions of an *all-powerful* reason. However, in *The Fatal Conceit* (1988) especially, we are asked to submit to the blind forces of tradition in the somewhat optimistic assumption that the private property and free market system would emerge, and be self-sustaining, almost by necessity. The familiar rights-structured, or even utilitarian-based, explanation for a free order seems to have been replaced by a Panglossian belief in the (possibly serendipitous) processes of social evolution. Rational justification for laws and institutions has given way to belief in the apparently benign forces of cultural evolution.

It would appear from this brief and necessarily selective account of contemporary social philosophy that the case for a genuine free market liberalism has not proved to be at all persuasive. It remains very much an 'unknown' doctrine, despite the collapse of communism and the spread of capitalism. The fact that nobody believes in communism any more does not mean that classical liberalism is understood, let alone attractive (it is certainly not 'inevitable', as the later Hayek seemed to imply). It is necessary therefore to reconstruct the doctrine in the light of contemporary social and economic thought: to indicate not merely its serviceability in the realm of public policy but, more importantly, to indicate its relevance to broader philosophical themes and, most crucially, to evaluate its answers to the abiding questions of the relationship between the individual and society.

Note

1. Some communitarian doctrines have conservative and traditionalist elements.

2. Ideology

Classical liberalism, as a normative doctrine, is an amalgam of a number of claims and its rationale rests upon a variety of competing intellectual foundations – 'scientific' economics, utilitarianism, natural rights, Kantian deontology, contractarianism and evolutionism, to name just a few. All of these differing intellectual structures may (though not always) generate a kind of convergence around a commitment to private property, free markets, limited government, constitutionalism and the rule of law. But do these beliefs constitute an *ideology*? Indeed, experience of politics in the 20th century can be used to justify the opprobrium that is so often attached to that word. However, to the extent that the doctrine does espouse a kind of world-view and, in the light of the fact that its explanatory tools have a more or less universal application, it is perhaps not inappropriate to call classical liberalism an ideology.

However, three important qualifications should be made here. First, unusually for an ideology, classical liberalism contains a heavy scientific component. Much of it derives from orthodox resource allocation theory of conventional economics and to that extent has some predictive value: the literature is replete with confirmations of the forecasts it makes about the likely consequences of, e.g., rent control, monetary laxity, and centralized planning. These predictions can be easily formulated in terms of standard Popperian methodology, i.e. as deductions from purported universally-true axioms (Popper, 1957). To the extent that these predictions derive from universally-true axioms they provide a necessary corrective to communitarian theories (and, indeed, liberal egalitarian theories) since the normative conclusions drawn from these doctrines have to be qualified by the conclusions of social science. The most obvious example is the erroneous distinction, derived from John Stuart Mill (1848), between the laws of production and the laws of distribution. Ignorance of the necessary connection between these laws has led liberal egalitarians to ignore the effect on efficiency that policies of social justice always has. As Robbins graphically put it, 'economics deals with the necessities to which human action is subject'

(1935, p. 26). The fact that a variety of social and economic systems are more or less compatible with these necessities should not be used to underestimate their force. Indeed, unlike physical laws, their effect can be resisted – but only for so long. Compared with the credibility of classical liberalism the scientific claims of Marxism are no more than pretensions which have been refuted by events.

The second qualification to the assertion that classical liberalism is a mere ideology is the argument that the doctrine's scope is necessarily limited. It does not provide an overarching theory of the good life; in fact it deliberately leaves the determination of ultimate values to individuals themselves. Indeed, in some versions its subjectivism about economic value is extended even to ethics; moral rules are mere devices to provide security and predictability to actors rather than expressions of higher value. These rules do, however, provide a framework for individuals to pursue a plurality of values. Also, ethical subjectivism is normally qualified by the argument that the rules of justice are not a matter of taste but have a certain objective necessity. They provide that security which is necessary if individuals are to pursue their differing conceptions of the good.

However, just how classical liberals can demonstrate the apparent objectivity of the rules of justice with a generally subjectivist approach to ethics will be considered below, but it is sufficient to point out that the doctrine's commitment to personal liberty precludes that 'completeness' which characterizes the ideologies with which we are familiar. Classical liberalism requires that questions about religion, art and certain types of private moral behaviour should be left to individual judgement. Nevertheless, classical liberalism does suggest decisive answers to certain *institutional* questions, even if it does eschew questions about ultimate value.

The third thing that differentiates classical liberalism from more familiar political ideologies is the most obvious, yet perhaps the most important. This is that it is not attached to a class, party or to any other collective group that might wish to use the state as a mechanism to implement its programme. For one thing, the individualism (both methodological and moral) that underlies it precludes the doctrine from any association with collective ends (except for those public goods which can be derived from individual choice, or at least individually-approved collective decision-making procedures). It is the individual, abstracted from social affiliations of the coercive type (though not those that accrue from voluntary agreements), that is to be liberated, not the group. And, furthermore, that liberation requires, if anything, a transcending of politics and a release from those restrictions that stultify the growth of individuality. Indeed, the variety of classical liberal positions, both in the foundational and the policy sense, indicates that the doctrine consists largely of philosophical and theoretical enquiries rather than of overt political dogma.

3. The Realism of Classical Liberalism

An additional contrast worth making with most other ideologies is that classical liberalism begins with a 'realistic' view of man and his condition. Certain features of the human predicament, although contingent rather than logical, are assumed to be more or less universal, e.g. the predominant (though not all-inclusive) motivation of self-interest, the permanence of scarcity, the infinite range of human wants and the lack of information that confronts all actors. While not denying that the particular form these features take will be influenced by a myriad of differing circumstances, classical liberalism does reject the claim that a change in circumstances will produce a change in man which will render the restraints (law, property rights, and so on) that are required to cope with these contingencies unnecessary. Following David Hume, and the other Scottish Enlightenment thinkers, classical liberalism deals with man as he is, not as he might be: as Hume (1953, p. 146) observed, plans of government which suppose 'a great reformation of the manners of mankind are plainly imaginary'.

Hence the reform proposals that the doctrine recommends are normally designed to correct the predictable effects of the working out of these contingencies. Most notable here is the Janus-like features of the postulate of self-interest: at one level, when it is subject to rules, it points to the possibilities of unforced co-ordination and the unintended production of the public interest, while on another its *unrestrained* operation leads to the classic social dilemma of the automatic production of effects that are destructive of that very same self-interest. Under certain circumstances, rational self-interest dictates that individuals will pursue courses of action that are harmful to themselves. Thus public goods which are desired by (almost) everybody can only be produced by artifice or contract, and not spontaneous processes. Yet as Buchanan (1975) has recognized, how do we stop the Humeian state, limited to the production of public goods and restrained by general rules, degenerating into the Hobbesian state, the unrestrained Leviathan that operates by *command* but whose very existence is the product of rational individual choice?

From its very beginnings, classical liberalism has focused attention on certain *descriptive* features of the human condition, and its normative recommendations have emerged from this analysis. There were, after all, markets already existing for Adam Smith to describe and there were legal orders before there was a jurisprudence to analyse them: all are phenomena that exist independently of man's will. In sharp contrast, one could hardly even imagine communist systems existing in the absence of Marx and the Marxists. Equally, though less dramatically, liberal egalitarianism depends on the same type of constructivism. Ironically, though, classical liberalism does also to some extent; not merely for the production of public goods (which are ultimately rooted in, or derive from, private desires) but also for those constraints on government which make the enjoyment of liberty possible. Markets can exist in orders which deny those non-economic aspects of liberty which individualists value. There is then, despite Hume and Smith's utilitarianism, a deontological strand in classical liberalism (Nozick, 1974) which emphasizes the necessity for these constraints, on individuals as well as governments, irrespective of their immediate consequentialist value (which cannot normally be calculated). Most classical liberals do value liberty for its own sake.

This specifically moral strand in classical liberalism is difficult to identify and occupies a somewhat shadowy position in its philosophy. This is not to say that Hume and Smith were not genuine ethical thinkers but it is true that their moral philosophy was, on the whole, *descriptive*, a sophisticated account of the ethical rules that had spontaneously developed to service a nascent property-based market order. Its claims to universality were always questioned. As MacIntyre (1981, p. 215) put it, 'its appeal to a universal verdict turns out to be the mask worn ... by those who psychologically and socially share Hume's attitudes and *Weltanschauung*'. Furthermore, throughout its history, classical liberalism has had to face the charge that the success of the market system that it described was bought at the cost of morality. Bernard Mandeville graphically, and almost enthusiastically, conceded the point with his claim that 'the grand principle that makes us social creatures, the solid basis, the life and support of all trade and employment without exception is evil' (1924, vol. I, p. 369). Virtue and commerce are forever in conflict and the moral rules that govern trade are no more than conventions that are necessary to make life predictable and secure for transactors. Still, as Adam Smith observed (1976a), why should that normal prudence exhibited in the market be thought immoral? And why should the rules of justice be thought antithetical to commerce?

I shall suggest that a morality understood as a form of convention is not necessarily condemnable, and that there are even universalistic themes within this approach. But the *apparent* moral lacuna in classical liberalism has encouraged its critics and has perhaps contributed to the mutation of the doctrine into liberal egalitarianism. It is a common theme in the post-communist world of ideas that the market has to be moralized by principles extraneous to it. It has encouraged sanitized versions of market economics, as in some theories of the social market economy, to emerge as correctives to the original doctrine; albeit at some considerable cost, not only in terms of adverse effects on productive possibilities which their implementation in public policy entails, but also in respect of intellectual rigour. One should not ignore the corrosive effect on free orders that the influence of such modifications has produced.

4. Spontaneous Order Theory and the Market

The scientific and ethical elements in classical liberalism are closely intertwined, even though its theorists have constantly affirmed the conventional philosophical position concerning the impossibility of deriving an 'ought' from an 'is', of demonstrating the compelling nature of moral judgements from any purported regularities in the social world. Indeed, this now accepted proposition was first formulated by David Hume (1972, p. 220), who nevertheless was both a firm believer in the claim that human behaviour was explicable in terms of regularities ('laws') and an early celebrant of the market system, and its associated order of property rights and the rule of law. His account of the connection between morality and causal explanation is relevant to contemporary classical liberal thought.

In his view, our moral judgements are derived from the passions, not reason; it is the former that drive us to action not the latter (which is confined to a calculative role, either in the realm of logic, or in empirical science). However, he was able to show that certain moral rules would develop spontaneously to service a liberal order and these are compelling not because they can be derived from some religious, or other metaphysical, foundation but because they tended to meet with men's *approval*. They are genuinely moral because they are normative guides to conduct which we are at liberty to ignore; but at a cost. Hence his rules of justice, which comprise basically the inviolability of justly acquired property and the obligatoriness of contract, although they are artificial, and irreducible to a metaphysical concept of natural law, are not *merely* conventional if that means alterable at will. He argues that 'though justice be artificial the sense of its morality is natural' (Hume, 1972, p. 221). It is their appropriateness for civilization and progress, and their consistency with certain unalterable features of the human condition, that justify a qualified claim for their universality.

This is the origin of the anti-rationalist foundations of classical liberalism, an approach continued, perhaps to excess, by F.A. Hayek in the

20th century. It is addressed primarily to that hubris in man which drives him to attempt improvements on quasi-natural processes; most commonly by the use (or misuse) of scientific method. The illusion that the elements of an economic, legal and moral order can be rearranged at will in order to generate some pre-determined outcome has been responsible for most of the catastrophes that are recurring features of the 20th century. The attempt to imitate the staggering success of the physical sciences in exact prediction, and more or less complete control over certain aspects of the environment, by social scientists has been one of the major reasons for these disasters. While one cannot ignore the malign effects of ethnic tensions and the resurgence of communal affiliations on the structure of social order (a fact which ought to dampen the enthusiasm of the communitarians to locate morality uncritically in 'given' communities), the urge of the rationalist to plan and direct events in advance of spontaneity is undeniably a main factor in the decay of civility and the decline of the modest predictability of rules. As Adam Smith observed, in 1759, of the rationalist,

> He seems to imagine that he can arrange the different members of a great society with as much ease as the hand that arranges the different pieces upon a chess board. He does not consider that the pieces upon the chess board have no other principle of motion besides that which the hand impresses upon them; but that, in the great chess board of human society, every single piece has a principle of motion of its own, altogether different from that which the legislature might choose to impress upon it. (Smith, 1976a, p. 263)

What is important here is the fact that because human beings have principles of motion of their own it does not mean that order has to be imposed, that no spontaneous order is possible, or that free actions produce randomness, disorder and inefficiency.

It is true that the history of Western political and social thought may be viewed as a kind of debate between the heirs of Hobbes, who believe that order is a product of design, that individual rational self-interest will produce chaos unless controlled by the terms of some contractual arrangement, and the proponents of spontaneity; but the presentation of this argument in either/or terms has confused the issue. There are, as most classical liberals concede, limits to spontaneous order. Indeed, it was Hume himself who pioneered the theory of public goods with his observation that, because people showed a natural tendency to prefer *immediate* satisfactions, a preference which can be destructive of their long-term interests, they construct social arrangements to correct this defect. In his view, government itself is the paradigm case of a public good (1953, pp. 39–42). There is little indication in Hume, as there is in Hayek (1988), that the blind forces of social evolution will somehow eventuate in a benign social order. However, the admission that circumstances may sometimes generate the necessity for a form of order that appears to owe more to rational design than spontaneity should not be used as a licence to dispense with those co-ordinating processes, both in law and economics, which have historically developed in the absence of a direct controlling will.

5. Market Orders

The painful experience in the struggle to establish market systems in former communist regimes is a tragic reminder of the long-term effect that wildly rationalistic interventions in gradually developing economic systems can have. Property rights, the rules of justice and the rule of law are difficult to re-establish in countries, e.g., Russia, where their nascent and inchoate emergence had been all but eliminated by collectivist planning. In such circumstances, a Hobbesian solution to the problem of order may be unavoidable. But even here it could be argued that certain sorts of rules and values would have developed spontaneously were it not for the imposition of rationally-designed orders. The theory of spontaneous order does rest ultimately on a moral claim to liberty.

There is, however, evidence, of a kind of moral vacuum, concerning the roles of liberty, justice and rights even in societies lucky enough to have inherited (at least partially) the kinds of economic and legal systems described by Hume and Smith. They seem to have instrumental value only and can hence be discarded if occasionally they fail to fulfil that role effectively. The reason why classical liberalism has been vulnerable to contemporary critics, who often call themselves 'liberals', is partly due to this problem and also because the theory of spontaneous order has been misunderstood even in that area in which it has been most effective, i.e., the explanation and justification of market phenomena. It is because of a misrepresentation of the market that critics of classical liberalism can claim the virtues of the exchange mechanism while rejecting most other features of the doctrine. They can be substituted with principles that do not derive from the universal elements in the market system. These principles are normally specifically anti-individualistic.

Thus, John Gray (1992, 1993) can rail against classical liberalism for its unsubstantiated claim to universalism, and unsustainable individualistic ethic, yet at the same time argue for the necessity of markets: 'The epistemic and the incentive arguments for the market are overwhelming' (Gray, 1992, p. 16). In his view the market is a cultural artefact and the form that it takes will depend on the social practices in which it is embedded. It is an error, he conjectures, to suppose that it is analytically linked to a concept of individual liberty (with its primarily anti-statist overtones of classical liberalism) detached and abstracted from particular forms of civil association.

Of course, there is a long tradition in economic thought, most noticeably in the various forms of market socialism, and in the recent appraisals of apparently alternative forms of capitalism in the Far East and in Germany, which does attempt to detach the market from its individualistic foundations. Most versions of this tradition depend on some attenuation of individualistic notions of property ownership, either by reference to straight collective ownership (somehow annexed to choice in the market) or to a version of communitarianism which places certain social responsibilities above individual gratification. In particular, all these non-capitalist doctrines, or severely modified versions of capitalism, are especially critical of the allegedly free wheeling, *laissez-faire* world of Anglo-American economies, inhabited by essentially *anonymous* transactors engaged in 'arm's-length' relationships and governed by formal, and minimal, laws only. This phenomenon is perhaps best exemplified in the market for corporate control where the takeover mechanism (Manne, 1965) determines, to some extent, economic change. It has been specifically attacked for the indifference to moral and communal values that it apparently generates. Almost all the rival market theories have this model in mind for their criticism. It is a model that would appear to have few ethical constraints on the pursuit of individual gratification.

The only specifically moral problem at this level (I leave aside questions of welfare and social justice until later) is the question of the legitimacy of certain actions that are involved in this method of co-ordination. The whole process may well have an overall utilitarian justification but does it not involve 'evil', in Mandeville's sense, since it seems to depend not merely on the elimination of communal, co-operative or altruistic motivations but, more importantly, on the exploitation of people's *ignorance*? Is one person not being used as a means to the ends of another and is there not therefore a breach of those deontological constraints on human action (which figure strongly in much classical liberal moral theorizing)?

Does not the inequality of information which characterizes all market processes breach rules of fairness? In a familiar example, does a potential purchaser of an apparently low-valued picture have to reveal to the owner that he happens to *know* that it is a Rembrandt? Again, does not the emergence of a monopoly by perfectly natural processes (and which could be justified as a reward for the superior foresight of a particular individual) damage unconscionably the freedom of those thereby excluded, in effect, from the market? It is considerations such as these that have powered the pro-market opponents of classical liberalism.

Still, despite these possible objections, emphasis still must be placed on the *creativity* involved in market process, a feature which is likely to be suppressed by an over-rigorous enforcement of deontological constraints. Creativity is necessarily involved since tastes are never given but constantly altering in unpredictable ways, and technological possibilities are not costlessly available but have to be sought out by *entrepreneurs* (Hayek, 1948; Kirzner, 1973, 1979) ever anxious to exploit the difference between resource costs and product price. Entrepreneurship does not have a supply price and therefore its features cannot be replicated by some central agency without its creativity being irreparably compromised. The contemporary attempts to detach the theory of the market from the elements of human action and freedom described in classical liberalism are redolent of Christian theories of the 'just' price, i.e. the long-run price of a product as determined by objective costs. But what creativity could there possibly be if a market system were subject to this constraint?

The assumptions about knowledge of costs that lie behind claims of market socialism (which hopes to dispense with genuine entrepreneurship) are remarkable but not dissimilar ones are made in the contemporary world by those who would impede the operation of market processes on behalf of communal values and expanded concepts of justice. Whatever moral values they may have are certain to inhibit those co-ordinating processes of market described by classical liberalism. The much vaunted communal versions of markets in south-east Asia do not eliminate entrepreneurship, although it no doubt takes a slightly different form there, least of all do they compromise the competitive instinct. As I shall show below, the German market economy is not quite like the Anglo-American one, but its apparent success does not invalidate the claims of classical liberalism. Evidence of creativity can be found in some superficially, unpromising examples of market processes.

Hence the claim that the market is a cultural artefact that lacks any universal application is misleading: it is the different *types* of market that reflect varying cultures. It is presumably the anonymity of Anglo-American economies, in comparison to the more intimate systems found elsewhere, that encourages their formalistic, indeed perhaps excessively legalistic, nature. The variety of market systems that we witness is not evidence of a lack of universality in the fundamental claims of the original celebrants of those orders.

None of this, then, dilutes the claim of Hume that rules of just conduct develop spontaneously and have a more or less universal application, or Smith's contention that the division of labour is the consequence 'of a certain propensity in *human nature* ... the propensity to truck, barter, and exchange one thing for another' (1976b, p. 25, emphasis added). Those who dismiss the universalistic claims of classical liberalism (e.g., Gray, 1989, pp. 239–64) have to explain how it is that regular patterns of behaviour reproduce themselves if individuals are accorded some freedom of choice, some space in which they can exercise individuality. Of course, this does not conclusively validate the doctrine (especially its moral component) but it does cast doubt on the argument that markets can *only* be understood in terms of particular traditions; as if there were no wider lessons to be drawn from the experience of property ownership and the practice of contracting. As long as rationality is interpreted in a minimalist sense, i.e., as a feature of human action which is concerned with the calculation of the means necessary for the achievement of self-determined human goals, it is a defining feature of individual endeavour. It is only when reason is understood in a maximalist sense, as a purely intellectual device divorced from experience, that it poses a threat to the utilization of knowledge and gradual adjustment to changing circumstances, which are both necessary for progress.

Especially important is the fact that the rules, e.g. of property, contract, and tort, that are necessary for the efficient operation of markets and capitalism have a claim to validity which is independent of specific enactment. Only in a trivial sense are these rules artefacts of society. They are, it is true, not 'given', as facts of nature like the weather, but are the products of human endeavour in a purely social context. However, this obvious truth should not mislead us into thinking that the forms of these rules depend solely on external social or political arrangements, that there would have been no commercial or property law in the absence of the state. The claim that all law necessarily depends on the state no doubt encourages the predominant view that commerce and the market exist somehow by permission of centralized authority.

This leads to the not dissimilar argument that the variety of particular markets and legal phenomena that we see in the world is a confirmation of the claim that their main elements have no claim to universality.

In fact, the literature is replete with studies of the spontaneous emergence of commercial law in the absence of the state (Trakman, 1983; Benson, 1990). Indeed, historically the state is a comparative latecomer: it came after both the law and the market. The myth of the priority of state is no doubt a consequence of the fact that obviously we know so much more about political events. Since the market emerged to serve the needs of unknown people, its development was a response to their very ignorance and its achievements were not the results of the will of a single person or body of persons, it is not surprising that it should have been underestimated as a source of human progress.

The claim that society or the state should regulate contract and property closely has, of course, some foundation in social theory and that foundation does not depend entirely on the argument that these institutions should somehow serve some higher collective (and contestable) purpose. It has often rested on the superficially plausible assertion that contracts are not self-enforcing, that the temptations of the moment may lead individuals 'rationally' to breach them, to the ultimate cost of their own well-being as well as that of society at large. In other words, without coercion, people may free-ride on the institution of contract, thus bringing about its ultimate demise. Even Hobbes could envisage the stability of instantaneous contracting, where the advantages of fidelity to agreements are immediate and tangible. However, he argued that any arrangement which required an element of trust would, under his assumptions, be self-defeating in the absence of an absolute sovereign.

However, modern social theory shows that this is not necessarily so; indeed if the Hobbesian claim were true one wonders how the common law (which preceded the state) could ever have developed. But as Robert Sugden (1986) has demonstrated, rules of cooperation can develop spontaneously. In exchange relationships individuals merely have to co-ordinate their behaviour in order to reap the benefits of cooperation. Communication between the participants and iteration of the 'game of callaxy' (Hayek, 1976, chapter 4) makes it possible for them to overcome the problems conventionally associated with collective behaviour. Furthermore, the exploitation of asymmetries, i.e., the gains that can be made from cooperation between individuals doing different things (as occurs in drivers following the rules of the road) increases the incentives for regularized behaviour. The fidelity to such rules and practices is reinforced by the development of the decentralized forms of punishment in which non-cooperators are excluded from beneficial participation – the tit-for-tat strategy (Axelrod, 1984). Co-ordination games are different, then, from conventional public-good phenomena.

It is true that cooperative practices are more likely to develop in small groups in which the advantages of cooperation are usually visible, and the possibilities of the detection of non-cooperators more easily available than in social situations with large numbers where genuine public-good problems occur. In these circumstances, a public good will be supplied whatever the actions of the participants so that the incentives to cooperate are dramatically reduced. Here there is obviously a role for a more formalized construction of constitutional authority.

Still, we should not discount the likelihood of cooperative attitudes spreading, in an evolutionary manner, throughout a society in the absence of political authority. In modern liberalism, the recognition of the necessity for political authority in one obvious aspect of social life has been used as a licence for it to dominate over areas in which voluntary behaviour has proved to be perfectly adequate. Furthermore, this extension has been primarily not to improve the mechanisms of co-ordination but to impose on free peoples particular end-states, or collective outcomes, which would not have occurred spontaneously. These endeavours have distracted attention away from co-ordinating phenomena that can occur spontaneously and are found wherever people are allowed some liberty of action.

6. The German Market Economy, *Ordo* Liberalism and Classical Liberalism

The failure to appreciate the underlying uniformity of market relationships, and the logical similarity of the rules that govern them, has led to the gradual detachment of the theory of market phenomena from classical liberalism and to the invention of a variety of adjectives that are now used to qualify the noun in the post-communist world. The *Soziale-Marktwirtschaft* (social market economy) is important in this context for two reasons. First, of all the alternatives to classical liberalism it is the only one that has a body of respectable theory and practice (in postwar West Germany) behind it, and second, not only was it specifically offered to the former East Germany, on reunification, as a superior form of economic organization to Anglo-American capitalism, but its influence is spreading elsewhere. There is, however, some confusion about the nature of the doctrine and its connection with classical liberalism. For although the phrase social market economy is used to describe an apparently distinct and specific form of economics, it is actually a somewhat protean expression that obscures more than it reveals.

The first thing to do, by way of clarification, is to distinguish between the social welfare (in the sense of state welfare) implications of German liberal philosophy from its genuinely theoretical components. Western Europe has had a long history of welfare interventions and German market theorists in the 20th century accepted their own Bismarckian inheritance with varying degrees of enthusiasm. Whatever originality German liberal theory had, it was not in its theory of welfare. The key theoretical question is how far the German theories of the market departed from classical liberalism, and whether the differences can offer any general insights into the nature of a free social order.

A distinction should also be made at the outset between the theory of the social market economy and *Ordo* liberalism (although there was some doctrinal overlap): the former was a sophisticated doctrine of a liberal welfare state, as theorized by Alfred Müller-Armack (1965, 1979), and, although it was far superior to the Swedish model, it was ultimately flawed (Hamm, 1989; Lenel, 1989) and eventually slipped into more or less orthodox social democracy. However, the *Ordo* liberals made some theoretically interesting critical observations of classical liberalism, almost all of which relate to the coherence of spontaneous order theory (Barry, 1993a).

The major theorists in *Ordo* liberalism were Eucken (1950, 1951), Röpke (1950, 1960) and Böhm (1960). As the title of their movement implies, their main concern was to demonstrate the conditions for social order (*Ordnungspolitik*), in its economic, social and legal manifestations. It is to be stressed here that what the *Ordo* theorists were trying to explicate was an order of freedom not welfare, although undeniably the latter was an incidental outcome of market processes and to be valued for that reason. The order of freedom was Kantian in origin, i.e. it was a proper legal order which made individual freedom possible, and which had contract and property at its foundation.

The interesting point is that these writers did not believe that the classical liberalism that I have been describing spontaneously produced the order of freedom. Röpke (1950, p. 119) wrote that: 'Like pure democracy, undiluted capitalism is intolerable', and Eucken (1951, p. 93) argued that 'experience of *laissez-faire* goes to prove that the economic system cannot be left to organize itself' and that it had to be 'consciously shaped'. It wasn't that Eucken rejected the underlying features of classical liberalism, indeed contract, tort, property and market relationships featured strongly in what he called the 'constitutive principles' of a liberal order (1950, pp. 80–121). His claim was that if it were left entirely to itself it would spontaneously degenerate. Intervention was not required to create a new and higher social morality, as the liberal egalitarians believe (as also did Müller-Armack), but, in effect, was needed to preserve the original individualist system.

Thus unlimited freedom of contract could ultimately lead to the decline of a contract-based society (Eucken in fact betrayed none of the distrust that modern liberals have for contracts and would no doubt have objected to the statutory-based, and sometimes judicially-derived, qualifications to that ideal) and to the development of *voluntary* market-closing arrangements that shut people out of the exchange process. He also feared that unrestrained *laissez-faire* would generate market power; people would be formally free but their actions would be causally-determined by others. Competition was a public good which had to be protected by the state, or more properly, in Böhm's view, by an effectively organized legal system which allowed individuals to sue for anti-competitive practices. Still, either way there was a general scepticism about the self-sustaining properties of unaided orders.

No doubt the Germans were influenced by the experience of their own country from the late 19th century until the end of the Second World War. Under the *Rechtsstaat* (rule of law state) Germany was more or less *laissez-faire* in economics (leaving aside Bismarck's social welfare state) but had experienced heavy cartelization and voluntarily negotiated market-closing arrangements between producers. Indeed, all this had been given legal validation by a notorious *Reichtsgericht* (Supreme Court) decision in 1897 which had upheld a market-closing contract; that led to a proliferation of similar ones (also German industry was governed by quasi-legal rules which could be said to have developed in a Sugden-like manner[1]). The *Ordo* liberals thought that these were phenomena to which all classical liberal orders were vulnerable.

Traditional classical liberals, for example Mises (1949, p. 346), were dismissive of these claims. Hayek was a little more elusive in his opinions. He was hostile to the social market economy; he described the use of the word social as an 'adjectival frill', or else it masked a substantive aim for a socially-determined redistribution of income (Hayek, 1967, pp. 237–44). However, he was by no means unsympathetic to some aspects of the philosophy of *Ordo* liberalism. In general, though, 'Austrian' economists were of the opinion that spontaneous market processes (especially the pressure of international competition) would gradually eliminate the imperfections that had themselves evolved naturally. Indeed, there is evidence that the problem of cartelization was exaggerated (Wallich, 1955) and that attempts to correct *apparently* market-closing arrangements by reference to imaginary perfectly co-ordinating models of perfect competition actually have adverse effects on those corrective methods that are automatically ('invisibly') operating anyway. It is probably true that the *Ordo* theorists were unduly influenced by American anti-trust law, which has a similar equilibrium theory at its foundation. It is also the case that they were equally concerned by the political effects that cartelization had, i.e. it was probably one of the factors that led to the rise of totalitarianism (at least it made it possible economically) in Germany.

In any event, it is difficult to see how *Ordo* liberalism (and the success of *Ordo*-inspired economic policies in the early years of the

West German republic) significantly dilutes the central claims of classical liberalism; especially the theory that social and economic co-ordination via rules has a universal application. The argument that the market is a cultural and social achievement is no doubt true in a trivial sense but the claim that it is a mere *artefact*, which can be altered or redesigned at will, without there being any serious effect on either co-ordination or the structure of individual freedom, is clearly false. The economic history of West Germany since the late 1960s, when the ideological implications of the social market economy began to have their effect, is ample confirmation of this (Giersch *et al.*, 1992). The enervating effects of excessive welfare legislation and other impediments to market adjustment to change and uncertainty are only just being realized in that country. Indeed, the *Ordo* liberals were early critics of some aspects of the social market economy. They would have little time for Müller-Armack's later claim that it would produce a new 'man' different alike from socialist man and capitalist man (Müller-Armack, 1965). For them, the features of man were pretty much universal.

If the contemporary critics of classical liberalism have the social market economy in mind as an alternative to individualism, and cite the success of (West) Germany as a confirmation of their argument, they are, in fact, mistaken. By all the measures of the reduction in liberty, e.g., rises in personal taxation, the proportion of GDP spent by the state, and the decline of personal responsibility for action brought about by compulsory welfare, Germany has become less of a free society as a result of the social market economy. Indeed, the *Ordo* liberals opposed most of these policies. Hence Gray (1992, pp. 82–3) is quite wrong (in his attack on classical liberalism) when he argues that 'the German case is the *only* one, so far, in which the role of government in the economy and in society has been radically, and seemingly irreversibly reduced'. He erroneously claims that this is a result of the social market economy. In fact, Germany is no different from other social democratic countries, public expenditure has risen from about one-third of GDP in the early 1950s to slightly less than half now (Giersch *et al.*, 1992, p. 132). This has mainly occurred through the implementation of the social market policies approved of by Gray (1992, pp. 73–89).

Note

1. These rules of industrial practice operated, apparently, without direct state enforcement.

7.   Law and Constitutionalism

The explanation of the spontaneous emergence of rules and practices that sustain a market order, and which have a certain universality, whatever *particular* form they take, is only one part of the classical liberal political philosophy. We live in a world which has seen a seemingly inexorable rise of the state and the apparent inability of constitutional constraints to contain this. The claim that liberal democracy would generate a genuine public interest, i.e. the common interest that citizens have in goods which have to be supplied collectively because of market failure, is no longer plausible. Modern democracies are driven by the 'vote motive' (Tullock, 1976) which produces electoral coalitions that redistribute income to groups necessary to secure their political power. Classical liberalism is partly a normative doctrine, concerned with the necessary features of a free society, and partly explanatory; it tells us how departures from the ideal occur.

This unending politicization of social life produces outcomes of high public spending and the successive attenuation of the rights of property and contract. They were probably not directly intended by the players in this electoral competitive game yet to some extent they were predictable. What we now have is de Jasay's (1985) 'plantation state', or form of political order by which government exists as a kind of entity in its own right; it prospers from the rents obtainable from politics. The periodic validation that government personnel requires from the electorate simply drives the system rather than provides any check to it. Since re-election normally requires the satisfaction of the demands of particular groups, the conventional democratic system provides no mechanism which effectively protects the public interest from the effects of group pressure. The US constitution, which at one time provided some constraint, has long since ceased to secure a protection for the core values of a classical liberal order.

This process has not only been driven by overt political factors but also by changes in the attitudes of judicial personnel. Thus in the US the constitutional defence of liberty, contract and property was formally abandoned in 1937 (Siegan, 1980) when the Supreme Court upheld a state statute that regulated wages. From then on, it consistently refused to protect economic rights and, in a case in 1938, officially endorsed the distinction between economic and civil liberties which has become the hallmark of modern, as opposed to classical, liberalism. That economic liberty is entitled to no constitutional protection in the way that personal and civil liberty has been officially proclaimed in liberal jurisprudence (Dworkin, 1977, pp. 277–8).

The search in classical liberalism for some kind of constitutional protection for economic liberty actually derives from an inchoate theory about the relative importance of ideas and interests in the determination of social events (see Barry, 1984, 1989). In the history of individualist thought one can detect a varying emphasis on either of these two factors. One strand of thought is concerned with the overwhelming importance of ideology and stresses that in the long-run it is ideas and values and not interests that are decisive: this was a view that Keynes and Hayek shared and Dicey (1926) alluded to in his account of the rise of collectivist thought in late 19th century England. He argued that 'public opinion' had been captured by spokesmen for this value system. They were influential on social legislation partly because they had managed to redefine liberty so that it was made consistent with what was, in effect, freedom-reducing legislation. Restrictions on contract (Green, 1888) were justified on the ground that they liberated individuals from their ephemeral and self-destructive desires. We can perhaps take this argument as decisive in the reformulation of liberal doctrine since it promoted an ideal of positive liberty which is significantly different from that notion of freedom as the absence of coercive law.

If ideas explain the way the social world works, then constitutional mechanisms hardly matter since it is presupposed that an élite is always able to influence decisively opinion and policy-makers. It could be mentioned in passing that it is difficult to see how Hayek could make this view consistent with his later public-choice-influenced constitutional reform proposals (Hayek, 1979, chapter 6), or with his evolutionism (a theory that purports to explain the flow of events independently of the human will). Ideas would presumably be ineffective in the face of such overwhelming social forces.

The interests theory is clearly more deterministic (though not necessarily materialistic): since it derives from economics it is likely to emphasize the fact that certain predictions can be made about human behaviour, subject to general explanatory laws and the specification of initial conditions. It is not concerned with celebrating the virtues of liberty directly in a moral sense but rather with specifying those institutional arrangements through which individuals' choices (including their preferences for public goods) can be maximized. There is a tradition in classical liberalism which is either sceptical of, or hostile to, the claim that morality can be objectively demonstrated. James Buchanan argues that public-choice theory is designed to avoid that 'retreat into empty arguments about personal values that spells the end of rational discourse' (1977, p. 82). The normative aspect of public-choice theory is concerned with the design of those procedural rules, agreement to which precludes or makes unnecessary moral argument about outcomes or states of affairs, or even about principles.

Can there really be a neutral, objective set of rules or is the familiar distinction between procedures and end-states a mere illusion? Does not every social theorist implicitly define the rules in such a way that the preferred outcome is generated anyway? Is it really enough to point out that under democratic politics redistributive policies reward particular groups rather than establish some purer ideal of liberal equality? As we shall see below a favoured classical liberal mechanism, the common law method of adjudication, has proved to be a less effective protective device for economic liberty than its theorists once thought. In such circumstances, argument about 'ideas' becomes unavoidable even if that is confined to the design of new institutional procedures so that the otherwise irresistible push and pull of group interests might be checked.

What *has* happened, however, is a virtual revolution in the theory of law that once prevailed in Western democracies: a transformation of the legal order which had been historically characterized as a body of *private* rules to enable individuals to fulfil their self-determined purposes, with a small area reserved for necessary *public* rules, into a directed system consisting very largely of public plans and purposes. The latter is largely decided by coalitions of groups which are themselves determined by electoral pressures. In its original form the common law system was an appropriate legal mechanism for the classical liberal order. Its appositeness can be seen in at least two ways: its structural features display the properties of a spontaneous order and its mode of operation is in conformity with the (limited) moral demands of the rule of law doctrine. Its general attributes enable both an efficient use of that limited knowledge that is available in any community and an economical use of necessarily scarce *moral* capital.

It is a spontaneous order precisely because its elements do not emanate from the mind of a single (personal or institutional) law-giver but emerge in an unplanned manner from the myriad of cases that have been decided and which provide precedents, and some degree of predictability, for actors in the future. In many ways, it is a formalized expression of those informal moral rules that naturally emerge to govern processes of social interaction. Thus formalized contract law arises out of the idea of a promise; property law confirms rights of ownership derived originally perhaps from some Lockeian-type claim to first possession or from morally legitimate transfers; and tort law governs the legitimate claims that individuals have when their interests are harmed. There is thus a combination of morality and formalized legality in common law systems. It should be noted, however, that even though codified systems look as if they were designed from first principles they are better seen as coherent declarations or summaries of what had developed spontaneously (though they do preclude that judicial creativity which is a feature of common law systems). No legal order can be designed *de novo*.

It is a fundamental claim of common law theorists that the compatibility (superficially, at least) of the common law and the market system should be obvious. The security provided by contract makes it possible for an infinite number of mutually-satisfying contracts to be completed, and the compensation provided by tort law ensures that no one is made worse-off by the competitive process. In theory, market exchanges under the common law are Pareto-improvements. Of course, that provides only the minimal foundation in morality because the Pareto-principle is notoriously silent on the distribution of resources from which mutually-beneficial exchanges proceed. Indeed, this is perhaps one reason why the idea of classical liberalism looks superficially less attractive than liberal egalitarianism. In some versions, classical liberalism provides no specific theory of *original* entitlement.

The role of the judiciary is crucial in common law systems: in essence it must preserve that overall rule structure which provides some degree of predictability for transactors. The judge does not proceed solely by deductive logic but he must construct an order of events which is socially coherent in the sense of preserving a kind of continuity. This can mean that new rules may occasionally be invoked in difficult cases. As Hayek says:

> Whether a new norm fits into an existing pattern of norms will not be a problem solely of logic, but will usually be a problem of whether, in the

existing factual circumstances, the new norm will lead to an order of compatible actions. This follows from the fact that abstract rules of conduct determine particular actions only, together with particular circumstances. (1973, pp. 105–6)

Examples of this can be found in the original spontaneous development of environmental law, where judges had to work out procedures for dealing with external effects (see Coase, 1960). It is not that the judges have complete discretion when the rules run out, as the legal positivists seem to imply, it is rather that their creativity is limited by a duty (which ultimately must be moral) to preserve an ongoing order. According to Hayek (1973, pp. 94–7), what judges are often doing is rendering articulate rules which were hitherto inarticulate, i.e. hidden in the interstices of a legal order. However, there is clearly a subtle interplay between discovery and genuine creativity in the determination of a legal order.

It might also be objected that the process necessitates an element of retroactive law since potential litigants cannot know what the law is until the judges have determined it. This is undoubtedly true, it follows indeed from the fundamental classical liberal epistemological claim that the amount of knowledge available to any person(s) in a society is limited; no designed legal order could ever anticipate exactly all future circumstances, and changes in events, which could give rise to litigation. It is, in fact, far more likely that it is the legislature that is capricious and unpredictable in its construction of new rules and, because of the vote motive, is less reliable in the production of law which is to the benefit of essentially *anonymous* agents in the social process. Furthermore, the stress on difficult cases obscures the crucially important fact that economic and social transactions constantly take place without ever being the subject of litigation. Disputed cases constitute a minute proportion of all rule-governed phenomena.

Of paramount importance in classical liberal jurisprudence is the distinction between law and policy: a distinction between the private rules that govern individual interaction and the public legislation under which government plans, addressed to specific social purposes, are conducted. The point of private rules is that they are, in essence, purposeless (Hayek, 1973, pp. 41–6), at least in the sense that they do not embody a public end, even though they may be given an overall justification in a utilitarian sense (however, their legal and moral *validity* would hold in the absence of this rationale). They are the necessary means for individuals to realize their self-determined ends and the rights they enforce have a Kantian justification, i.e. it would be wrong to violate them on behalf of some public policy and they must be fully universalizable. Public law is supposed to emanate from public bodies charged with the responsibility of implementing plans, and these agencies are subject to democratic accountability (inadequate though that invariably is). In a country like Britain, in which legislation from a sovereign parliament takes precedence over all other claims to law, it was inevitable that public law should triumph over private law in circumstances of majority-rule democracy. Still, those countries with formal constraints on law-making power cannot be said to have fared any better in the protection of liberty or in the preservation of traditional common law procedures.

However, the problem in classical liberal jurisprudence lies not merely in the failure of constitutional constraints alone (though that is crucially important) but in the spontaneous feature of the common law itself. The theory holds that we cannot predict law's development, or even evaluate it from any external standpoint. We can only appraise it with the standard set by the internal coherence of the structure as a whole. From this perspective, it turns out to be merely a contingent fact (though clearly not fortuitous) that the development of the common law served the needs of an ideal classical liberal order. The judicial search for consistency, coherence and the universalization of rules so that they can apply to future unknown cases is by no means the same thing as the sustaining of an order of inviolable property and contract rights. For example, logically almost any rule can be universalizable so as to satisfy the Kantian requirement, and clearly not all universalizable rules are limited to the protection of property and contract. Even Hayek himself admits (1973, p. 89) that developments in English common law (especially landlord and tenant law) in the 19th century were not conducive to an orderly market society. Law here required corrective action by legislatures, or by innovative judges breaking with legal tradition.

What is more disturbing is that in the 20th century deliberate judicial intervention in common law processes has been, if anything, disruptive of its co-ordinating processes; it has not been aimed at correcting inadequacies in the legal servicing of a free order, as suggested by Hayek, but rather it has steered the legal order away from this. And this has occurred quite apart from, and in addition to, the depredations brought about by direct public intervention. The shift in the meaning of liberalism from its classical and individualistic foundations towards a social or egalitarian form has certainly been helped by a change in the judicial attitude, a phenomenon which itself is a tribute to the potency of ideas in social life.

America is the best example of this transformation since there the judiciary is to some extent constitutionally protected from politics and has the constitutional authority to resist the legislatures. For much of America's history the Supreme Court upheld the economic rights of the individual, in contract especially, against statute (formerly from the states but later from the Congress also). This protection derived from judicial interpretation, along Hayekian lines, since the Constitution does not *specifically* make contract inviolable: however, the Fourteenth Amendment's due process clause implicitly required that a special reason be produced if the economic liberty of the citizen were to be lawfully abrogated. Originally the Court demanded very special reasons for the permissibility of statutory constraints on contract.

This all ended in 1937 with the *West Coast Hotel* v. *Parrish* case. From then the Court began to uphold every economic regulation and every taking of property (Epstein, 1985). Not only that but it has extended civil liberties, notably in the areas of affirmative action (sometimes justified as a form of compensation to certain disadvantaged groups so as to make the procedural rules more neutral), expanded the rights of criminal suspects and widened the scope of civil disobedience; much of this has been achieved without the aid of legislatures. Of course, some of the Court's activity here might be made consistent with classical liberalism but what is clearly not compatible with the doctrine is the supposed asymmetry between civil and economic liberties which has now become an established feature of American law, and which was invented by the judiciary.

The irony in all this is that the turnaround in judicial behaviour has been justified by a jurisprudence that bears an uncanny resemblance to Hayek's apology for common law reasoning (and its evolutionary development). I refer here to the legal philosophy of Ronald Dworkin (1977, 1986), one of the foremost spokesmen for liberal egalitarianism. Like Hayek, Dworkin objects to a certain kind of legal positivism that reduces judicial activity to the strict reading of statutes (and other legal materials). A legal system cannot be exhaustively defined in terms of rules but must be understood as an ongoing order which must include moral principles if it is to provide some security and certainty for the participants in a social process. However, this morality is not derived from some rationalistic notion of natural law detached from actual legal practice but is embedded in the traditions of an established legal order. For Dworkin, like Hayek, interpretation of principles is required if the main elements of the rule of law are to be preserved.

In the positivist model of law, judges have strong discretion when the rules run out, and this inevitably means that a considerable amount of retroactive law, hence unpredictability, is probable since it is impossible to forecast how judges will act. In contrast, Dworkin argues that in 'hard cases', where there is some doubt about which rule to apply or where there is no rule at all, judges do not call upon considerations extraneous to the legal order but invoke principles which are a part of law, even though they are not mechanically applied, as rules customarily are. This looks very similar to Hayek's distinction between non-articulated and articulated rules; the former, though not fully expressible in formal legal propositions are essential for the judge in his endeavour to provide a more or less predictable order of events. Similarly, Dworkin argues that judges have to call upon principles if law is to retain its integrity and autonomy. For both Hayek and Dworkin, judges discover the law.

Dworkin openly concedes that judges must, to some extent, be political theorists: 'Law is deeply ... and thoroughly political. Lawyers and judges cannot avoid politics in the broad sense of political theory' (Dworkin, 1985, p. 146). However, he is careful to point out that this theorizing is constrained, not merely by written and uncontroversial law, but also by the fact that in searching for principles the judges are doing no more than bringing to the surface values which are partially submerged in the history and practice of a legal community. In a famous case, *Riggs* v. *Palmer*, decided in 1889, Dworkin shows how the principle, 'no man shall profit from his own wrongs', was used to deny inheritance to someone who had murdered his grandfather (even though the formal rules of inheritance were apparently satisfied). Later examples of the invocation of principles are much more controversial, indeed they are overtly political, but Dworkin insists that the principles which judges draw upon are not their personal values or ideologies. A system of law is to an extent neutral, and the answers it provides to difficult cases are objectively-determined by the defining elements of the order itself.

Furthermore, Dworkin makes a crucial distinction between principles and policy. In a jurisprudential division of labour (which has great philosophical significance) the legislature has the responsibility for advancing collective goals, while the judiciary protects those rights which are validated by principles. Under a written constitution, which specifies (however inarticulately) rights, the legislature is constrained only by those rights. Even in a system like Britain's, which has no formal constitutional document, Dworkin (1986, pp. 23–9) still maintains that common law adjudication must be conducted in the light of principles which underlie the system and which give correct answers in hard cases – if only the judges would see them.

Yet, from a jurisprudential position that is close to Hayek's, Dworkin has managed to produce a legal philosophy that stands opposed to the basic foundations of classical liberalism. Dworkinian judges have successively generated in America a series of decisions which have, in fact, implemented the social agenda of modern liberal egalitarianism: affirmative action (ostensibly to correct past injustices), forced integration of schools through busing arrangements, some substantive equality and in other areas where controversial decisions seem to be neither sanctioned by the Constitution nor by the non-articulated rules that underlie it. Worst of all, economic liberty apparently has no legal protection at all, since it is 'a silly proposition that true liberals must protect economic liberty as well as intellectual liberty' (Dworkin, 1977, p. 264). Or, as he insists elsewhere, the familiar civil liberties. The grounding for this (arbitrary) distinction is, presumably, that regulatory and other interventionist economic *policy* does not infringe civil rights, it does not compromise a person's right to 'equal concern and respect' (Dworkin, 1977, pp. 272–8) as discriminatory law based on race or sex does, or measures designed to curb freedom of expression do.

Of course, in Hayek's jurisprudence, the role of the judiciary is to preserve an ongoing legal order and in this activity no categorical distinction is made between economic and civil liberties. This is a more plausible understanding of a legal order for it is surely an emasculation of a predictable rule-governed process to imagine that it should only protect individual civil liberties when people's well-being is just as much a function of their economic opportunities. Those whose economic prospects are adversely affected by interferences with contract and excessive regulation, or whose property rights (as in America) are severely attenuated by public authorities' perverse use of the takings clause, surely have their rights violated just as much as those who experience arbitrary racial and sexual discrimination undoubtedly do.

The shrinkage of economic rights is perhaps even more important than the expansion of civil liberties. If there are no limits to regulation then there are clearly reduced opportunities for creativity in the market. The freedoms to experiment, to innovate and to upset existing arrangements, are vital aspects of the epistemic function of the market, i.e. its ability to co-ordinate dispersed knowledge. Even if these considerations are dismissed as being too crudely utilitarian (there are deontological strains within both liberal egalitarianism and classical liberalism which doubt that anything of specifically *moral* value can be inferred from the market's mere success in satisfying desires) it is not difficult to show that the exercise of economic rights is just as much a feature of a person's freedom as is the possession of civil liberties. Limitations on the right to contract or on the pursuit of the career of one's choice because of arbitrary licensure laws (most often passed by state legislatures at the behest of politically powerful special interests) are deprivations of liberty in the fully-fledged moral sense precisely because they put collective goals (dubious though they usually are) ahead of individual self-expression. Anyway, even Dworkin's right to equal concern and respect is vague enough to encompass economic rights, even if he has other reasons for rejecting them.

Still, it is not clear that all this involves a legal methodology which is all that far removed from Hayek's evolutionary jurisprudence. As has already been noted, the US Supreme Court's pre-1937 upholding of some economic liberties depended on a certain kind of creative judicial activity. Neither Hayek's nor Dworkin's accounts of legal procedures can be truly neutral. Both are influenced by the kind of society which they say the law should preserve. How can we possibly say which is the more authentic description of a legal system when each permits judicial innovation in order to sustain and nurture the integrity of the *law*? Once we start down the evolutionary path, and refrain from substantive evaluation of outcomes, our critical faculties are necessarily blunted and rival states of affairs and competing judicial decisions can claim fidelity to the legal process.

The twists and changes in judicial behaviour which have characterized Western legal systems in the 20th century (especially America's) are no doubt to a great extent a product of changes in ideas. Judges do seem not to want to limit their role to preserving a traditional notion of legality, or the modest replenishing of end-independent rules, but are just as anxious to shift an otherwise self-sustaining order in a particular direction. Though how far their behaviour can be understood, in a manner suggested by public choice, as a subtle response to political and electoral pressure, is an arguable point. Would the resuscitation of the classical liberal legal order require a rational reconstruction of law, via a constitutional revolution which entrenched economic liberties (and hence reduced the need for judges to play the kind of role Hayek recommended), or would it merely require a change in ideas? It is not at all clear what the classical liberal answer to this question is.

Perhaps a first step in the theoretical reformulation of classical liberal jurisprudence would be a recognition that a legal system can never be neutral between differing ways of life. Although it does permit a wide degree of liberty of choice for people to pursue their varying conceptions of the good, liberalism is itself grounded in a cultural tradition that already upholds this pluralism. This is the kernel of truth that lies in reasonable versions of communitarianism. To say this is to attenuate slightly classical liberalism's claim to universalism. But it does not eliminate it. Since much of formalized law is the codification and declaration of those rules that Hume identified as being essential for civilization and progress, its existence is a response to more or less universal needs.

None of this is meant to deny that legal systems can perfectly well exist that do not embody specifically classical liberal features, and Hayek is therefore wrong to imply that his conception of law is the only valid form and all others are aberrations, but it does suggest that the freedom and prosperity associated with them are by no means accidental. Indeed, the difficulties associated with the establishment of markets in former communist countries are largely the result of the obliteration of legality that occurred under communism. The differences between Hayek and Dworkin are not reducible to sterile linguistic arguments concerning the use of the word law. The issue is: Which of their conceptions is more supportive of a free society? Dworkin's arbitrary exclusion of economic liberty from legal protection makes his model of law inadequate for countries struggling to emerge from totally controlled economic systems.

The claims of liberal egalitarian legalism are, in fact, much more ambitious than those of classical liberalism for, in effect, they involve the universalization of what have become peculiarly American conceptions of liberty and equality under law. The very fact that such ideas are highly controversial even in the US is enough to suggest that the prospect of their exportability to communities struggling to create, or recreate, the basic elements of legality is virtually non-existent. Liberal egalitarianism takes on a definite ideological form when it presents itself as intrinsically right. It is, in fact, no more than a rationalization of a rather special form of legal order. To demand that economic liberties be given the same legal protection as civil liberties is hardly ideological: it is a recognition of necessity.

A further observation, which applies to classical liberalism and to liberal egalitarianism, is that both doctrines seem to be associated with, indeed encourage, forms of order characterized by *excessive* legalism. This phenomenon is a consequence of the fact that liberalism has historically been associated with the idea of an *abstract* society: a form of order in which essentially anonymous agents are held together by general rules. It would not be true to say that liberal society is a loose collection of strangers held together by abstract rules alone since its pluralistic structure does encourage voluntary forms of association in which more intimate social ties are given full rein. But the recourse to law to settle disputes is a feature of it that is less noticeable in other societies (such as those of south Asia), which, nevertheless, strongly feature the market, private property and competition in their social arrangements. It seems highly unlikely that the Western model (Hayek's extended order) is one to which evolution is driving all societies, as he seems to imply in *The Fatal Conceit* (1988, chapter 1).

It may be the case that excessive legalism is both costly (in straight economic terms) and socially divisive (in that it deters the emergence of non-formal dispute settling) but it cannot be wished away by idealistic communitarianism. It seems to be an inevitable feature of a certain type of open liberal society. Also, it is an especially distinctive feature of liberal egalitarian legalism which, because of its construction of more complex, substantive and contentious forms of liberty and equality, creates more opportunities for litigation. If judges could have restricted their role to one of maintaining a predictable order of events, and restricted their innovative activity to the repair and maintenance of this, it is less likely that a liberal legal order would have mutated into the complex and unpredictable morass that it has become.

8.   Constitutionalism and Sovereignty

The major part of classical liberal legal theory has been addressed to the problem of containing the growth of government. The aim has been to subject it to rules. This is a crucial aspect of the rule of law but the tendency in the modern world has been for governments to evade its strictures. It has even been a claim of some classical liberal theorists that if government could be fully subject to the rule of law then there would be no need to rely on substantive, and therefore controversial, notions of natural rights, or disputable economic ideas of 'efficiency', in the evaluation of government's performance. We would simply have to question whether its activity was lawful. If the standards were strict enough considerable protection of personal liberty could be guaranteed. The criteria of lawfulness would require that rules be perfectly general, that they name no person or group, and that they be non-retrospective in application. It would be logically possible to make liberty-reducing laws consistent with these criteria, but their existence, and fidelity to them by legislatures, would constitute some constraint on government. Of course, classical liberals would also demand that a set of rights, determined by agreement, be specified in a constitution, but questions of appraisal then would not be about the intrinsic value of those rights but whether government activity had been in conformity with their requirements.

Experience has shown that constitutionalism of this type has been a rare occurrence in history. Constitutions have not only been compromised by the vagaries of judicial interpretation in more or less stable societies, but the very idea of constitutional constraint seems to be alien to all but a few countries. If a culture of constitutionalism is a definitive feature of classical liberalism it, in a curious way, damages the doctrine's claim to universalizability. For order would seem to be a product of social phenomena other than the formalized rule-following implied by liberal constitutionalism. Indeed, it would not be too far from the truth to say that societies can only make constitutions work if they already have the social attitudes that recognize the necessity for governmental restraint and which understand the meaning and value of individual rights: in which case they would not need the paraphernalia of the separation of powers, judicial review and written guarantees of liberty and equality. Britain managed to preserve economic and personal liberty for a very long time when it had, at least since the 18th century, the ideal recipe for absolutist government, i.e., a Hobbesian sovereign parliament limited by nothing other than the customs and practices of restraint which were 'internalized' by its governing class. A further irony here is that British constitutional arrangements, which include most importantly the superiority of (parliamentary) statute law over common law, were a product of spontaneous evolution; they were neither planned nor even thought of by any known person or body. That they were at one time benign but later malign is sufficient to make us at least sceptical of the argument that an explanation of social development in evolutionary terms has an automatic connection with classical liberalism. Of all the elements in classical liberal theory, constitutional order is the one most likely to need explanation by rational constructivist methods, i.e. satisfactory political rules are more easily understood and evaluated in terms of specific agreement than as the almost random products of evolution.

The claim that governmental restraint depends almost exclusively on cultural conditions and that there is little need to call upon constitutionalism is, however, misleading. The form of political rules a stable community has makes a crucial difference to the outcome of the political process; it surely wasn't simply that the US was a stable society throughout its history (with the obvious exception of the Civil War period) that guaranteed (until 1937) its market economy and private property system: it was as much to do with the particular constitutional form of the separation of powers and judicial review. Again, the slide towards collectivism in Britain, which began in earnest after 1945, was obviously hastened by parliamentary sovereignty, operating to some extent irrespective of particular movements of general opinion. A further indication of the difference that constitutions make is revealed by the fact that under sovereignty systems it is easier both to establish and to reverse collectivism, while under more complex political arrangements government intervention can be resisted and delayed to some extent but it is more difficult to undo once established.

Classical liberals have historically not been prepared to take the kind of risks that sovereignty involves: risks that have become transparent with the rise of majoritarian democracy. As Hayek observed (1978,

p. 86): 'The triumphant claim of the British Parliament to have become sovereign and so able to govern subject to no law, may prove to have been both the death-knell of both individual freedom and democracy.' Sovereignty, because it authorizes absolute legislative power, is in breach of the rule of law: a doctrine that presupposes that all agents should be subordinate to rules not of their own making. Britain could not have a formal constitution (at least prior to the country's entry into the European Community) because the rules that govern the political process are made by the actors in that process. A rule of the constitution, e.g. electoral law, has no greater significance than a routine piece of road traffic legislation. It is extraordinary to imagine that political actors would bind themselves, yet that is what the British system asks of them.

It is true, in strict jurisprudence, that parliament cannot determine the 'rule of recognition', i.e. the fundamental rule of a legal system that determines validity (Hart, 1961, chapter VI; Barry, 1993b) for it is that rule which authorizes parliament and distinguishes genuine law from bogus claims to law. But the British fundamental rule is extraordinarily permissive. Given the obvious fact that parliament does not even represent a genuine majority, let alone a wider body of opinion that would morally be required to validate changes that seriously affect people's rights and liberties, it would be odd to suppose that it would reflect the public interest, where that refers to laws or policies that concern people as members of the public rather than as members of private groups. As public-choice theory predicts, power is exercised on behalf of particular interests that can be aggregated into organized parties. Under parliamentary systems, a not very demanding electoral test is required for the exercise of sovereign power.

Despite its complex constitutional arrangements, the position of the US is little better, at least with regard to economic matters. Judicial review, which is so powerful a constraint in the area of civil liberties, is almost completely absent in the economic field so that the Congress might just as well be called sovereign here. The historical record of 'parchment' (Wagner, 1993) documents in restraining political power is dismal, certainly in the 20th century. This must largely be due to important changes in the emotive appeal that certain political concepts have undergone in the last few decades, especially democracy.

9.   Liberty and Democracy

At one time in the 19th century there was a genuine fear among liberal theorists of the dangers that unrestrained majority rule posed to traditional liberties, including property rights. The naïve hopes of Bentham and James Mill that democratic institutions would maximize utility, once the 'sinister interests' of the landowners had been replaced by the common interests of everyone else, were successfully countered by the dire warnings of Lord Macauley and (to a slightly lesser extent) John Stuart Mill. But their forebodings related only to the possible overt 'tyranny of the majority', not to the insidious effects that vote-maximizing behaviour would have on the long-run structure of law and on the genuine public interest. Only Sir Henry Maine, in his *Popular Government* (1885), showed an awareness of the damage that 'wire-pullers' and parliamentary manipulators could do to the inherited structure of predictable rules. This, rather than straight tyranny, has proved to be the great threat to long-term economic order.

In the 20th century, however, the imprimatur of democracy has been sufficient to sanctify almost any act of government. The vote-maximizing process makes it rational for actors to generate policies that favour short-run redistributive activity by government, yet popular opinion validates that in the name of democracy. The market system, private property and, indeed, constitutional order itself are public goods which no one has an interest in promoting. Still, there is undoubtedly a subtle combination of the influence of ideas and interests at work here since the immense appeal of the democratic idea has underwritten the corrosive effects of more or less unrestrained group politics. One suspects that only a combination of a change in ideology and some institutional rearrangements can repair the defects in conventional democracy.

If paper-thin constitutional rules have been so ineffective in restraining politics is there any other mechanism that can perform this necessary function? One aim might be to exploit the possibility of political competition itself. Choice between competing political parties within a political regime could perhaps be extended to choice between regimes themselves. An availability of the 'exit' option for individuals dissatis-fied with government might drive political authorities to keep taxation down and regulation lighter simply to avoid losing their clients. This was an idea originally suggested for local government by Charles Tiebout (1956) but it is in principle extendable to wider political authorities. If governments cannot be hemmed in by parchments then perhaps the natural process of competition could be an effective substitute. There is a nice parallel here with monetary competition, if rules cannot provide stable money then choice in currencies (Hayek, 1978) is perhaps the only alternative; though inflation will presumably have to be well-advanced in any domestic economy before a mass exit from its cur-rency occurs.

Of course, very high costs will be incurred by individuals leaving one state to join another, more favourable one. But the idea is the essence of federalism; the existence of several states (under very sim-ple general rules), each of which allowed free entry and exit, would provide that mechanism for a wider expression of subjective preference for various forms of government action. However, the federal idea itself has been badly damaged in the 20th century with the rise of uniform standards across a national territory. This has the effect of reducing exit opportunities. In the US it was perhaps given the final death-knell in a controversial Supreme Court decision in 1985 (*Garcia* v. *San Antonio Transit Authority*) in which it was ruled that the federal element con-sisted only in the fact of the states' representation in the Congress; even the paper-thin constitutional protection offered by the Tenth Amend-ment was judicially expunged.

The experience of the European Community (Barry, 1993) is instruc-tive here. Originally, the practice (since 1966) was for individual states to veto proposed European-wide legislation emanating from the Coun-cil of Ministers. The requirement of unanimity undoubtedly prevented the imposition of uniformity across states. But, as public-choice theory predicts, this had efficiency costs: small states held up the implementa-tion of otherwise desirable policies, notably the single market, the removal of trade barriers and the abolition of exchange controls. Hence the introduction of qualified majority voting in 1986 across a range of issues overcame the blocking tactics of some member states. In theory it was a fine example of normative public choice.

In practice, however, it has turned out rather differently. It has led to a growing uniformity of law across Europe in relation to social policy, the environment and labour practices. Those member states that could exploit competitive advantages by offering different standards have been bought off by inter-regional transfers. Furthermore, the European Court of Justice has tended to uphold all the important legislation from the Council of Ministers, even when that appears to be in conflict with fundamental European constitutional documents. There is a quasi-liberal constitution in Europe (primarily the original Treaty of Rome, 1957) but it has been of little avail. In any case, it is far too vague a document to function as a clear restraining instrument. Matters will only get worse with the Treaty of Maastricht (1993) since the range of issues subject to qualified majority voting has considerably widened under it. The opportunities, and incentives, for member states to exit from European law have been reduced, therefore the advantages of that strategy for individuals has been almost eliminated.[1] If political competition is to be an effective method for protecting liberty, a change in both ideas and institutional arrangements will be required.

One should not, however, completely despair of the possibilities of international political and economic competition reducing the effects of national and transnational sovereignty. The opening up of the world in the post-communist age has increased the pressure on national governments to relax their hold on their citizens. The greater mobility of capital and labour is steadily reducing the costs of exit for individuals. This is already producing the 'imitative effect' (first suggested by Hayek) of successful liberal capitalist orders: the idea of markets is spreading. In the face of a growing internationalism, even the controls introduced under sovereign constitutions might turn out to be less than decisive.

Note

1. This has led to just that kind of 'sclerosis' which was a feature of the British economy in the 1970s.

10. Liberty

To account for the emergence of a spontaneous market order and to explain the nature of the legal and constitutional rules that sustain it is only one aspect of a normative political theory. It has been a temptation for some classical liberals to avoid investigation of the moral properties of a free society, largely because these are regarded as too subjective to be admitted into rational discourse. It has been claimed that reason is incompetent to adjudicate between rival claims to virtue and must be confined to a more readily calculative role in the determination of those institutional conditions which are necessary for the maximization of whatever values individuals may hold. Even in so complex a moral theory as David Hume's, morality could be said to be only a little more than a sophisticated version of prudence. Lurking behind all this is Mandeville's cynical claim that commerce necessarily involves an abandonment of virtue. Classical liberal writers have, nevertheless, been anxious to maintain that liberty is to be valued not merely as instrumentally valuable for the production of social utility but as a necessary element in individual well-being; following Kant, it is maintained that individuals are not to be used merely as means to the ends of society. As Nozick says:

> ...there is no social entity with a good that undergoes some sacrifice for its own good. There are only individual people, with their own individual lives. Using one of these people for the benefit of others, uses him and benefits the others. (1974, pp. 32–3)[1]

This is a clear contrast with Benthamite utilitarianism where individuals disappear once their preferences are incorporated into a utilitarian calculus, in the construction of which interpersonal comparisons of utility are permitted. Freedom here depends solely on the permission of the sovereign.

It is a commonplace feature of liberal social theory that the diversity and subjective nature of human values precludes them being incorporated into some objective maximand which government is under a duty to promote. Not only does this not accord with a realistic view of how markets work (the dispersed nature of knowledge and the ever-changing nature of preferences makes it impossible for a benevolent legislator to determine such a maximand) but it also, and perhaps more importantly, drains the exchange system of intrinsic moral value.

It is to be noted that this objection is just as much addressed to authoritarian regimes that nevertheless permit free markets as it is to collectivist orders that forgo all the advantages of economic freedom (or to heavily-controlled economic orders that may nonetheless allow the conventional social liberties, rare though these are). The authoritarian examples do allow economic liberty, and this permission at least gives them some value, but it is not strictly *moral* liberty. The emerging market economies of south-east Asia, and especially China, would seem to fit this description only too well. The 'illiberal' regimes that practice this economic freedom have no doubt recognized the advantage of decentralized exchange but the driving force of this recognition of them is a simple and crude utilitarianism. The participants in such orders are, in principle, being used as means to socially-determined ends just as much as the unfortunate victims of fully-collectivized economic orders are. In the tradition of classical liberalism, liberty cannot be broken up in this way but is a principle to be used in the evaluation of all aspects of social life. Furthermore, although the tradition of liberty permits a plurality of individually-determined goals to be advanced, freedom is not simply one concept among many, that can be traded away, say, for the advancement of social justice (Barry, 1965, chapter 1), but is more properly described as part of the liberal order of procedural justice in which *fundamental* values do not compete.

The classical liberal theory of liberty involves a substantive moral claim; it is not merely a semantic analysis of the concept. If it were the latter it would have nothing to say about the obvious fact that liberty can only be enjoyed in a rule-governed context in which the liberties of some are restricted by the rights of others. If I have the liberty to accumulate property then others are under an obligation to respect it; they are forbidden from trespassing on my land or stealing my goods. This obvious fact has led some writers (Cohen, 1979) to object to a classical liberal (and broadly negative) account of liberty, i.e. one that understands freedom as absence of constraint. In Cohen's view, capitalist legal institutions which protect the property of a minority, necessarily render the proletariat, who own nothing, unfree. Any theory of liberty must therefore include an account of the permissible constraints on human action. If the law justifiably prevents others from using my property this must be because I have a *right* to freely exchange with others, to inherit, or to act on my choices in an uncoerced manner. In other words, protective laws allocate liberty rights, even though their existence does legitimately reduce the liberty of some in a formal sense.

What has to be maintained here is that a legal system that protects this right to liberty increases liberty overall. After all, the only alternative to private ownership of goods is some version of a theory of the common consumption of them; as if some fair rule could be imagined that allocated their use and which forbade exclusive possession. This is, in a sense, a feature of genuine public goods but any extension of this arrangement to ordinary goods and services on the ground that it maximized overall liberty is most implausible. All forms of ownership restrict the use of valuable objects but an examination of history reveals that a wider spread of ownership is achieved under liberal capitalism. In fact, Cohen is simply in error when he claims that law merely protects the liberty of a minority. The undoubted existence of unequal ownership is not evidence of the absence of a general liberty right. Under collective ownership the right to restrict use is simply transferred from individuals to a public agency. This is not an increase in liberty. Indeed, many classical liberals say that the existence of property is an absolute guarantee of liberty against the state. This is not historically true since there are examples of oppressive regimes preserving property rights. Still, private property is a necessary condition of liberty, if not a sufficient one.

Of course, it could be argued (Steiner, 1974) that liberty cannot be increased or decreased overall, it is only distributed in varying ways across individuals. This seems, however, to ignore the probability that a general system of law does increase liberty overall by providing that security for individuals to maximize their well-being. Though comparisons in liberty-enhancing terms between legal systems are difficult it seems rather odd to suggest that a fully-planned social system merely redistributes liberty (it is, of course, true that the planners have a great deal of liberty) rather than reduces it overall. What we look for in a legal system is how far it increases the range of available choices to individuals even if that does, as it must, reduce some choices of others. A system of general and predictable rules, which reduces direct commands to a minimum, is surely freer overall than the chaos and unpredictability of a regime subjected to ephemeral orders from the centre.

Still, we should not identify liberty with mere choice: after all a person under threat technically chooses; he prefers one alternative to another, no matter that conditions have been so manipulated that the choice is almost inevitable. It was this feature of human action that enabled Hobbes to claim that liberty and determinism are compatible. However, we do say that freedom is attenuated when the range of options available to an agent has been reduced. Threats backed by sanctions clearly reduce the range of options. This does not dispose of the problem because it is still possible to argue that market exchanges can be coercive, especially in economic depressions when available employment opportunities are narrowed, and that some intervention might be said to increase overall liberty (or, at least, redistribute it more fairly). It is true that in such circumstances the *value* of liberty is not particularly high but it still remains a controversial question as to whether state intervention, by purporting to increase opportunities, also increases liberty. It might be more proper to speak of such action as being designed to maximize a disputable conception of *welfare* (which is quite another thing). To say that people's liberty increases when their powers or capacities increase is to embark on a highly misleading course since it implies that there should be no limit on the permissibility of government activity. Almost any action can be justified on the ground that it is liberty-enhancing merely because it somehow maximizes power or capacities. A person's liberty, however, is increased if an oppressive law is relaxed, irrespective of the difference that is made to his or her powers or capacities.

Yet a full understanding of liberty requires that we take some account of the *value* of the choices that are available to people. The extent of liberty cannot be known solely by a kind of quantitative assessment of the choices available to them merely because of the absence of law. They must be important choices. In an intriguing example, Charles Taylor (1985) claims that a purely negative view of liberty is implausible. Albania, he argues, could be said to be a freer society than any in the West because it actually had fewer constraints on personal action, e.g. no traffic laws or the range of minor (and not so minor) constraints that are a feature of capitalist liberal democracies. Of course, there were severe restrictions on highly valued activities in Albania but these prohibitions were few in number.

It is, however, not at all clear that Taylor's example is especially damaging to the classical liberal conception of liberty. This doctrine does attach moral importance to liberty and does make discriminations between various liberties (though it does not accept the arbitrary distinction often offered between economic and civil liberty) in accordance to how they advance individual well-being. A lack of liberty to acquire property would be a reduction in overall liberty even if it were accompanied by fewer restrictions elsewhere. It would be absurd to deny that the market does expand liberty; it does this, not merely by satisfying people's subjective (and possibly ephemeral) desires but also by providing conditions for the formation of life-plans independently of government. And classical liberals want to assess morally the various liberties by reference to how far they enable persons to advance their own conceptions of well-being. On this criterion, laws in Albania were oppressive despite their (apparently) narrow range.

Furthermore, the argument that markets can coerce, because they sometimes do not present a wide range of choices for disadvantaged individuals, obscures the fact that freedom is normally reduced by identifiable agents: impediments to liberty are those which are the alterable and intentional actions of persons in political authority, or those who in some other way are able to determine particular outcomes. The market, although it is the product of the actions of innumerable agents, is not itself a coercive body to which we can attribute the normal notion of responsibility. It does not 'act' in any meaningful sense of the term.

This slightly modified concept of negative liberty as a right against unjustified coercion has come under attack not merely because it appears to reduce the range of coercion narrowly to political authorities but also because it is claimed to be inadequate at its foundation. It is argued that it does not properly describe what it is to be free since it makes no determinate suggestion as to what is valuable in life. We must be free for a reason and the purpose of that freedom is not revealed merely by the absence of law. Gray (1992), following Joseph Raz (1986), argues that freedom can only be understood as *autonomy*, where that seems to mean the possibility of individuals choosing from as wide a range of options as possible: 'It is patently obvious that autonomy is far more than the mere absence of coercion by others, since it is self-evident that that condition may co-exist with a complete inability to achieve any important objective or purpose' (Gray, 1992, p. 23).

It might be thought that this is simply a demand for redistribution to increase people's capacities, so that liberty becomes valuable to those hitherto unable to enjoy it, and indeed his suggestions for an enabling welfare state (ibid., chapter 5) are consistent with this project. But it is clear from his other work that Gray has a more ambitious conception in mind. In 'What is Dead and What is Living in Liberalism' (Gray, 1993, pp. 282–398) he appears to prefer a form of human flourishing which is by no means reducible to the satisfaction of subjective desire and he claims that a liberal order is deficient if it precludes the idea of 'perfectionism'. In other words, there are collective goods, quite unlike the public goods of subjectivist classical liberal theory, which have intrinsic value, i.e. they have worth even in the absence of anyone expressing a want for them. It is argued that autonomy 'presupposes as one of its constituent elements a rich public culture containing a diversity of worthwhile options' (Gray, 1992, p. 42). Raz is even more openly favourable to the idea that persons can express liberty and morality only as members of particular social groupings that embody the idea of the good: 'A person can have a comprehensive social goal only if it is based on existing social forms, i.e. forms of behaviour which are in fact widely practiced in his society' (1986, p. 308). Naturally, the specific significance of coercion diminishes in this perfectionist context; indeed Raz (1986, p. 417) subverts the standard liberal argument by suggesting that for a state not to provide the conditions for autonomy would be harmful and liberty-reducing for some people.

Gray and Raz are not adopting some kind of positivist account of liberty which would involve highly controversial concepts of rationality and the (possibly) coerced pursuit of a higher end, an approach of which Berlin (1958) was so rightly critical. Their conceptions of liberty are consistent with pluralism to the extent that they identify freedom and autonomy as the ability to choose from a variety of ends. However, the model of choice exercised in the market place would seem to be a morally inadequate understanding of freedom because it maximizes subjective choices rather than intrinsically valuable things. Though Gray does concede that the market does encourage some freedom as autonomy.

What are we to make of all this? Some would perhaps quibble a little at Gray's apparent linking of freedom with welfare in his suggestion that an uncoerced person who lacked resources would not be genuinely free. It is a commonplace in classical liberal thought that freedom is not the same as wealth. But I do not think that that is crucially important. It is true in a sense that a person's liberty can be constrained by a lack of resources and, as long as liberty is not *identified* with capacity or power, no confusion results from conceding this: although purists would still maintain that in such circumstances it is the value of liberty that is reduced rather than liberty itself. All societies, including classical liberal ones, develop a variety of ways of dealing with the victims of, say, genetic misfortune or unpredictable economic change. Indeed, Gray's critique of the contemporary welfare state's solutions to such problems is conducted in impeccably classical liberal terms (1992, chapter 6); although his own particular version of an enabling welfare system is far from classical liberalism. Also, both Raz (1986, chapter 9) and Gray (1992, chapter 6) are highly critical of conventional egalitarianism.

The real problems occur with the concept of autonomy itself and the dismissal of negative liberty as empty or meaningless. It is simply not true that the absence of coercion is not itself a value independently of a consideration of the ends and purposes that an individual may pursue. The fact that one is not coerced means that whatever is done is a product of choice, irrespective of whether it is directed to one's long-term ends, the value of which may be in dispute. There is surely some value in the fact that in a free society opportunities exist for individuals to be authors of their own actions. The demand that they should be widened is not empty or meaningless.

It is possible to say that a person acted freely even though he or she did not act autonomously in the rather rarefied sense described by Raz and Gray. It is not that absence of coercion is merely a condition for the exercise of autonomous choice. Negative liberty is not merely instrumental. People can and do protest about unjustified limitations on their liberty irrespective of the projects they wish to pursue. In fact, they may not even know them. A free society, with a vibrant market economy and a predictable legal order, is the only social arrangement in which people can come to terms with their ignorance: and lack of information here refers not just to economic knowledge but also to one's personal plans and projects. One cannot know what it is to be an autonomous agent until one has experience of freely choosing amongst alternatives. And this requires that each individual should have a sphere immune from the intrusions of coercive law. It is not that autonomy defines liberty but rather that one has to be free before one can be autonomous. To define liberty exclusively in the context of given social forms, as Raz appears to do, precludes the moral legitimacy of a person breaking out of those forms. The innovator (perhaps regrettably for a conservative) succeeds largely because he or she upsets existing social arrangements.

None of this is meant to imply that there can be human agents completely abstracted from social forms who are understood solely through the calculus of their desires (that would be to discount fool-ishly the value of spontaneously developing social rules and practices), nor is it meant to endorse the kind of mindless and deliberate non-conformism recommended by John Stuart Mill. However, it does rest on the idea that under conditions of non-constraint, individuals are the makers of their own lives, whether or not they lead them as fully autonomous agents. To accept that individuals are necessarily under-stood partly by their social natures is not to endorse the moral priority of social forms.

One can go further and challenge the importance of autonomy itself. Many people (Kukathas, 1992, pp. 101–14) lead their lives unreflectively, they follow traditional rules and practices and they make choices of a fairly trivial kind. To what extent are they unfree? Like everything else which is valuable, autonomy has an opportunity cost, the time and other resources needed to acquire it could be spent on something else. One could complain about people's foolishness in not becoming au-tonomous (they may indeed become willing victims of consumer fads and fashions in market society) but not their lack of liberty if they behave in an uncoerced manner.

The real issue in all this for classical liberalism is the enhanced role for the state in the creation of conditions for autonomy. Raz (1986, p. 161) may dismiss as unimportant the taxation (which he distin-guishes from coercion) required to preserve a common culture and things of intrinsic value, but others would not. It also involves the state, through its officials, deciding what is valuable and worth cherishing. As a matter of historical record, the efforts of purely voluntary actions in these areas is probably better than the state's. However, the matter becomes much more disputable when Raz appears to give the state not just authority in autonomy-promotion, he also imposes a *duty* on it: 'The government has an obligation to provide an environment provid-ing individuals with an adequate range of options and the opportunities to use them. The duty arises out of people's interest in having a valu-able autonomous life' (1986, pp. 417–18). Making the state responsible for the correction of low autonomy is a somewhat exotic example of its response to market failure.

Among the many difficulties with this position is the obvious fact that autonomy is an indeterminate moral ideal; it is not like rights-protection or the supply of public goods, which, although controver-sial at the edges, are capable of being formulated as reasonably coher-ent tasks for a state to perform. And although Raz is insistent that the autonomous life involves choice between alternative projects he is equally convinced that market-based individualist society is incapable of fully meeting this demand. Why not? The answer is, apparently, that this order, because it is based on subjective choice, will fail to provide objective and intrinsically valuable goods; notably the maintenance of common forms of life. But since there is likely to be considerable disagreement about what these intrinsically valuable ends are, the state, in selecting one or more out of the range of possible candidates, is likely to generate the very tensions that undermine common forms of life. Although Raz's pluralism precludes the state promoting and privileging any *particular* way of life, it is difficult to see how the authority he grants to the state would not be used in this way.

An individualistic, rule-governed social order does not preclude the development of common forms of life, indeed they are likely to emerge and be sustained spontaneously precisely because they are the unintended outcomes of individual interaction under general rules of law. Intrinsically valuable goods, such as a common culture and an artistic and scientific tradition (although they must ultimately be subjectively valued by human agents) can be treated as 'objective', rather in the way that literary works can be subject to informed discrimination, quite independently of their probably low and certainly unreliable market value, without in any way departing from the basic tenets of traditional liberal society.

A final problem with entrusting the state with too great a role in the promotion of autonomy is that this aim can and does compete with other values. Perhaps the costs in terms of taxation to pay for this is not excessive, although neither Raz nor Gray suggests any procedural device to keep this within reasonable bounds, but it does nevertheless involve a loss in negative liberty for those compelled to pay. Although Gray (1992, p. 88) argues that public spending could be reduced to 25 per cent of GDP if the welfare state were reorganized by methods that would advance his conception of liberty as autonomy, the very indeterminacy of the idea makes this wildly optimistic. He seems to think that the lessons of public choice do not have a more or less universal application and he argues that a society which develops a moral code that enjoins the open political discussion of public issues would generate more effective constraints on government spending than the cold, formal rules recommended by classical liberal theory. No evidence is produced for this proposition, which could quite properly be described as wishful thinking. To entrust the state with the responsibility of autonomy promotion while not providing formal checks on its activities here is almost certain to lead to a loss in overall liberty.

Note

1. Although Nozick (1989) has departed from his original social philosophy.

11. Contractarian Liberty

The strictures of Raz and Gray as discussed in Chapter 10 identify some difficulties with the classical liberal theory of liberty and its account of the defining features of a free society. It does sometimes involve the attempt to derive a theory of freedom from the basic propositions of economic theory, notably those concerning rational choice and subjective value, without reference to any *background* of morality. It is true that one tradition of classical liberal thought has been deeply sceptical of the truth-value of ethical statements (even of the *meaningfulness* of moral discourse itself) and has suggested that the subjective evaluation of goods in the market place is in fact the appropriate model even for normative or moral statements. All types of evaluation are rooted in individual choice. In fact, this normative individualism is not quite the same as technical ethical subjectivism or scepticism since these latter positions reject the ultimate validity of any moral claims (including individualism). However, since the important feature of classical liberal subjectivism is its denial of the existence of transcendental moral standards the difference in nomenclature is not significant. The important question is whether the value of liberty, and the institutions of a free society, are sustainable in subjectivist terms alone.

The approach is clearly linked to the contractarian tradition in social thought. This presupposes that ethical values are generated by rational individuals out of a context which is essentially non-moral. Freedom consists in the fact that the values emerge entirely from the choices of individuals: the moral and political order in which they live is a product of their actions and no person or entity has a licence to impose any form of society on them, even the conventional free society of markets and the rule of law. The institutions of a liberal order have no intrinsic value and whatever moral worth they have is solely a function of their being chosen. As we shall see, this raises serious problems for the transition to free orders from existing unfree societies, for the conditions of the status quo may be such that few would voluntarily opt for conventional liberalism. Indeed it may be irrational (in the economist's sense) for them to do so.

James Buchanan (1975, 1977) is the most sophisticated exponent of this general methodology. His meta-ethics are basically Hobbesian but he hopes to show that a limited state, and not a Leviathan, can be generated by the same motivations as those assumed by the great pessimistic philosopher of authoritarianism. In a rigorous anti-transcendental stance, Buchanan argues that all truth, be it ethical or anything else, rests entirely on *agreement*. He says that: 'Truth, in the final analysis, is tested by agreement. And if men disagree there is no truth' (1977, p. 113) and, 'Fairness, as an attribute of rules, is defined by agreement; it is not, and cannot be, defined independently of agreement, or at least of conceptual agreement' (1977, p. 130). Thus negative liberty, and the institutions that protect it, are only valuable if they are what people actually want, since any attempt to go beyond their preferences would be to 'play God'. This could, and does, lead to a kind of stultifying conservatism, although it is based on unconservative, individualistic premises.

These, then, may be thought to be unpromising propositions on which to found the idea of a free society. However, by using devices such as the state of nature and the social contract (Buchanan and Tullock, 1962; Buchanan, 1975) Buchanan shows how its main institutions would be constructed out of people's choices, unencumbered by traditional ethical trappings or communal notions. It is an entirely abstract demonstration. Notice also that his approach is purely *procedural*: there are no pre-existing ethics of fairness or justice which would be discovered if only people could be detached from their real-world predilections and temptations.

There are no limitations, derived from a supposed objective morality, on what may be agreed. On leaving an imagined (or real) Hobbesian state of nature people will construct a Protective state, an authoritative agency for validating property titles and enforcing agreed-on law, merely to economize on defence. They can make Pareto-improvements on the state of nature, because the latter involves wasteful expenditure on private protection. They will generate such a rule-structure to protect their property: but, in advance of the Protective state, both production and predation are equally valid activities as claims to property. There are, then, no exclusive Lockeian natural rights to resources. The constitutional contract must be agreed unanimously if it is to be legitimate. However, there are provisions for less-than-unanimous decision-making rules in the delivery of (subjectively-determined) public goods. These procedures are designed to overcome hold-out tactics that would be employed by minorities under unanimity. However, what makes such rules legitimate is that they would be agreed to unanimously in the original contract. It is quite likely, though, that the rules for the production of public goods would be stricter than those that prevail in contemporary majoritarian democracies.

This sort of reasoning, whatever its limitations, has at least one clear lesson for classical liberal theory. That is, institutional arrangements are a product of people's choices, they cannot be left to evolution since there is no 'invisible hand' in society, as there is in the market, to harmonize desires. All our rules, institutions and practices are capable of improvement (Buchanan, 1977, p. 38) and to submit to the blind forces of tradition would be a tame admission that people are not the makers of their own futures. The hypothetical scenarios that Buchanan constructs are devices to highlight our present predicament and to suggest alternative futures. But all recommendations must be made under the *imperium* of the rule of agreement. It would be a breach of that principle if a state of affairs (no matter how intrinsically desirable from a classical liberal perspective) were to be imposed on a status quo which contained individuals who did not subjectively value it.

It might be doubted that there is anything moral about all this. At the most, it appears to be an exercise in prudence: people adopt rules which will advance their interests, and the rules, because of the requirement of agreement, will provide universal and non-discriminatory protection. However, no conditions are laid down which ensure that they will be liberal rules. It is certainly true that Buchanan does not see morality in terms of having the right motivations: it is a matter of following rules which may, on occasions, not be in our short-term self-interests. Indeed, his whole structure is designed to overcome prisoners' dilemmas, which are endemic to all societies.

Still, one quintessentially liberal feature remains: that is the fundamental requirement of *consent*, not only to the (hypothetical) foundation of government but also to changes that may be proposed to actual forms of political authority. However, the moral force of this requirement is immediately diluted by an absence of discussion of the circumstances that accompany consent. As in Hobbes, agreements are agreements and we are not to discriminate amongst them according to the conditions in which they are made. At first sight, Buchanan appears to have added little to the Pareto principle of welfare economics, he has simply (albeit interestingly) found a new application of it. Just as the Pareto principle is silent on the distribution of resources from which trading begins, Buchanan is ethically mute about the facts that precede political agreement.

Yet the purely procedural aspects of this makes the possibility of criticism and change in existing society limited. This is because of the pivotal position of the status quo in Buchanan's thought. Although it does not have intrinsic value (as an orthodox conservative might suppose), it is where we start from and it constrains any changes we might wish to make. It is the 'whole set of rules and institutions at any point in time' (Buchanan, 1975, p. 77) and change from it has to be by agreement. Thus, whereas a moral theorist of negative liberty might wish to protest at freedom-reducing action by government (on the ground that it adversely affects individual well-being or abrogates the moral right to exchange) irrespective of questions of procedural legitimacy, Buchanan can only suggest constitutional reforms which would better protect individuals' enjoyment of valuable things already acquired. And such reforms must be unanimously agreed to.

In fact, the status quo is systematically ambiguous (Barry, 1986). It could either prohibit change, on the ground that some people would be harmed by it (which makes it Pareto-inefficient) or permit it, despite the harm, because previously agreed-on rules authorize governments to take action. The introduction of a classical liberal order to replace a collectivist status quo is both condemnable, because it would override the preferences of those who benefit from the prevailing state of affairs, and permissible because the rules of change allowed it. Either way, ethical debate has to be conducted in substantive terms and in it the value of liberty will not depend on mere agreement. In other words, morality must be *prior* to constitutional arrangements, crucially important though these are for a free society.

Buchanan implicitly recognizes (albeit reluctantly) the necessity of adding some moral notion to the conventional apparatus of economic theory. He is a firm believer in the doctrine of the moral impermissibility of using individual agents for collective ends: 'In my view, democratic values must be founded on the basic Kantian notion that individual human beings are the ultimate ethical units' (Buchanan, 1977, p. 244). And he is firmly opposed to those welfare economists who try to construct imaginary end-states of perfect co-ordination independently of the actual choices of individuals. But despite these deontological gestures it could be argued that Buchanan has only presented a purified view of economic methodology. He has saved economics from the perversions of utilitarianism but reinforced its scientific, morally neutral, integrity. This, however, would be an unjust final verdict, not only because agreement and subjective choice must feature as necessary elements in classical liberal doctrine, but also because in his stress on the importance of deontological rules there are the beginnings of a much-needed moral theory. As he says in *The Limits of Liberty*: 'Something other than the utility function employed by standard economic theory must be introduced to provide an explanatory foundation that legitimizes individuals'... claims to stocks actually produced by their own efforts independently from the interference of others' (1975, p. 63). But he gives no clear indication of what this is. It seems to me that it can only be a notion of negative liberty that focuses on individuality and rights and which has a moral force that circumscribes mere agreement. It is a morally-justifiable framework of rules and procedures designed to protect a *pre-existing* moral right to negative liberty.

12. Justice

The current dominance of liberal egalitarianism over classical liberalism is intellectually upheld by a subtle transformation of concepts that are common to both doctrines. Thus the individualistic force of classical liberal thought, its commitment to law, rights and personal liberty has been retained by egalitarians but only at the cost of giving these terms a pronounced collectivist, or at least redistributivist, twist. Examples of this exploitation of an apparently unavoidable permissiveness in political language are legion. It is justice and rights that provide perhaps the best examples of the process. That notion of moral equality which is at the basis of any liberal theory of justice has now been converted into a demand for economic equality so that the original injunction to treat people equally, under common and impartial rules, has been supplemented by the argument that they ought to be 'treated as equals' (Dworkin, 1986, pp. 295–6). And this demand can only be met by a substantial redistribution, either as justified compensation for the disadvantaged or as the rather bald demand for equality as a good thing itself.

In John Rawls's theory it is morally unacceptable that people's well-being should depend on the 'distribution of wealth and income … determined by the natural distribution of abilities and talents' (1971, pp. 73–4) since individuals do not *deserve* these abilities and talents. They are the outcome of a 'natural lottery' which has no ethical rationale at all. Similarly, Dworkin (1981) distinguishes between inequalities which are endowment-sensitive (the product of the 'brute luck' of nature) and those that are sensitive to ambitions and efforts. Only the latter are acceptable since they are the results of actions to which the normal liberal credo about personal responsibility for action is relevant. In both Rawls and Dworkin, that income and wealth which accrues from unjustified possession of either inherited resources or from the 'luck' of natural talents constitute a kind of unowned pool which ought to be redistributed by reference to social (or philosophical) principles.

It never occurs to theorists of social justice that there may be *undeserved* entitlements, claims to assets to which neither merit, desert or need have any direct relevance. Many market exchanges produce incomes which it would be difficult to say were deserved in any conventional sense but they would still be legitimate under conventional notions of entitlement. And inheritances, of course, are the prime example of unmerited, windfall gains. Yet there are rules which establish title, whether to the products of productive labour, exchange or gifts. There is no manna from heaven available for redistribution; inherited wealth must have been created by somebody's productive efforts, and that person had a right to pass it on to whomever he or she chose. If theorists of social justice are to treat all assets as constitutive of a collectively-owned pool, to be redistributed according to principles different from those that govern the creation of these assets, they face an impossible task unless they also wish to abolish *all* accepted rules of entitlement.

However, the new doctrine of social justice is superficially subtler than old-style egalitarianism largely because it builds on (or exploits) some familiar ideas in classical liberal theory, namely the right to ownership of resources and the meaning of equality. More importantly, it could be said to have taken to extremes a popular idea in classical economics, the theory of rent. In the last century some orthodox market economists were a little disturbed by the phenomenon of rent, i.e. income derived from the lucky possession of a scarce resource that had no alternative use. What they had in mind was land. Since its earnings are conventionally not the product of entrepreneurship, it was said that they could be taxed away (or some socialized form of land ownership introduced) with no, or only a negligible, effect on productivity. Contemporary theories of social justice are based on a similar idea; that people do not own their natural talents in the way that landowners were thought to have no right to their land. Although they are not utilitarians, both Rawls and Dworkin are concerned about productivity. They have to be, since the least advantaged or the victims of brute luck must be financed (compensated?) from the 'unjust' earnings of the arbitrarily advantaged. There must therefore be incentives for individuals to create this surplus. There is, then, some justifiable inequality.

However bizarre some of the foundations of the new redistributionism may sound, they have a clear resonance for contemporary theories of justice and this has at least compelled classical liberals to flesh out their criticism of the doctrine of egalitarianism with more considered concepts of the self and of ownership. Arguments are less intense now about the adverse aggregative effects of redistribution (although it would be fatal to ignore them) and more about what a morality uncontaminated by crude utilitarianism means. Most importantly, an analysis of justice enables us to understand more clearly the differences between the ethics of liberty and those of equal liberty.

Classical liberal theories of justice are 'backward-looking' in that they are concerned with the past: how people were treated, how wealth was acquired and what actions generate what entitlements are the typical questions asked. This is perhaps why legal justice is the closest to a correct use of the concept (though this should not be identified with positive law since existing legal systems often embody injustice). In contrast, social justice is typically forward-looking. Even though it is not often utilitarian it does demand that society be reorganized so that morally better states of affairs are produced. Furthermore, classical liberal theories of justice distinguish it from whatever other virtues a society might display, such as benevolence or some notion of the good. What is distinctive about justice is its obligatory nature: it is permissible to enforce justice while the other virtues are often thought to be supererogatory (desirable but not compelling). One of the reasons redistributivist theorists use the concept of justice rather than straight egalitarianism or socialism is because they wish to capture its special urgency. We may not go as far as demanding that justice is *absolute* but we require extraordinarily good reasons to evade its dictates.

It is the backward-looking nature of justice that gives it its universal appeal. It is a minimum requirement of morality that punishment should be related to conduct, that people are entitled to equality before the law and should be given their 'due'. Of course, there can be disagreement about what some of these things may mean in practice (Aristotle insisted that like cases be treated alike, but that begs the question about what are like cases). However, if there is any kind of generic moral code it would consist almost exclusively of these features. By contrast, social justice seems a peculiarly Western concept, not universalizable but conditioned almost exclusively by developments in 20th century Anglo-American and West European political philosophy. In an important way, while being obligatory, justice makes few (positive) demands on us. As Adam Smith said: 'Mere justice is, upon most occasions, but a negative virtue, and only hinders us from hurting our neighbour' (1969, p. 160).

Closely allied to this negative conception is its moral individualism: an important argument is that we attribute the words just and unjust to the actions of identifiable persons and not to mysterious social forces. As Hayek says: 'To speak of justice always implies that some person or persons ought, or ought not, to have performed some action; and this 'ought' in turn presupposes the recognition of rules which define a set of circumstances wherein a certain kind of conduct is prohibited or required' (1976, p. 33).

Thus to complain that a distribution of income is socially unjust is to presuppose that it was determined by a human distributor whose actions can be morally appraised. Yet the distribution of income thrown up by the market is the outcome of the actions of innumerable individuals, not one of whom intended any particular pattern. The distinction between procedural justice, or the rules that govern individual action, and end-state justice, particular patterns of income and wealth, is vital here because classical liberalism holds that any attempt to freeze a pattern (irrespective of the desirability or otherwise of the chosen distribution) must involve the violation of procedural rules and the freedoms and equalities they embody (Nozick, 1974, p. 164). The market is in constant flux and to track it so as to generate and preserve social justice would make impossible demands on our knowledge, as well as increasing coercion in society. Much of contemporary social justice is powered by a quite erroneous distinction between the laws of production and distribution. This quite arbitrary distinction assumes that there is no feedback effect on production whatever distributive policy a government chooses. However, productive possibilities are not fixed but are very much influenced by how the social pie is sliced up.

It is to be noted that this account of procedural justice says nothing specifically about the role of government beyond a prohibition of its enforcement of particular end-states. A welfare state is not a priori excluded, for there may be good reasons why aid to the disadvantaged should be a legitimate state function; even though in existing welfare states the redistribution is largely a consequence of interest group pressure and has little to do with equality (Le Grand, 1982). Still, classical liberalism tends to hold that public welfare derives from benevolence rather than from the strict duty of justice.

Despite this, there may still be an argument that the state's welfare responsibilities ought to be dictated by justice rather than by benevolence or a general social duty. Raymond Plant (1991) argues that though particular outcomes of a market process are unintended they are foreseeable and that justice is as much a matter of how we respond to its victims as it is about individual behaviour under rules. In other words, justice is not entirely a backward-looking concept and injustice can occur through acts of omission as well as acts of commission. While there is obviously something to this argument, in the same way as we might say that a refusal to help someone in distress on the ground that there was no contractual obligation to do so was in a way an act of injustice, it does not affect the main thrust of the procedural theory which really objects to the *whole spread of incomes* being determined by principles, such as need and desert, which are external to the market itself. Plant's argument does not establish the case for social justice, which is normally not limited to the problem of individuals in distress, even though it might well compel classical liberals to reconsider the *duties* implied by the pure theory of procedural justice.

There are, however, some problems with the classical liberal theory of justice. For one thing, is it simply utilitarian, as Mises (1962, p. 34) certainly thought? Is the objection to social justice merely that continued interventions in the market so distort the incentive structures facing rational agents that everybody in the long-run is made worse off? Hayek, of course, claims quite rightly that he is not a utilitarian in that a firm opposition to the possibility of interpersonal comparability of utilities underlies his rejection of constructivist end-states (Hayek, 1976), but his approach is redolent of a certain kind of consequentialism. His whole endeavour is to show how the decentralized exchange system best exploits the earth's resources, and copes with a niggardly nature, so as to generate a kind of progress: no matter how abstract and indeterminate this is. There may even be a tension between his theory of the purpose-independent rules of procedural justice, which could have a Kantian foundation in their respect for persons, and his theory of the wealth-generating features of market process which has no necessary connection with abstract morality.

Since no independent source is given for the moral rights that attach to the participants in a market process there is something of a lacuna in the ethics of classical liberalism. Entrepreneurship is unquestionably an essential mechanism in the co-ordination process but does the profit, payment above marginal productivity, which it generates have any moral justification? It may be highly dangerous economically to suppose that it could be taxed away with no loss in productivity but as long as its justification is purely instrumental, the inequalities the profit motive creates will always provoke moral strictures derived from social justice.

It could be argued that the rules that govern market relationships are the rules of co-ordination rather than of justice. As already noted,

Buchanan claimed that justice is what is agreed upon. Unlike Rawls, who believes that rational individuals under certain conditions, notably including ignorance of their present circumstances and the future value of their talents, would agree on particular rules of justice (which include a specific distribution rule). Buchanan argues that *whatever* they agree on is itself just. Since Buchanan's contractors have knowledge of themselves and others, and have acquired holdings in an anarchistic equilibrium, there is little possibility that the resulting agreement will be Rawlsian. All that we can say is that to ensure predictability a set of constraints on a potentially destructive self-interest will be imposed. But are these the rules of a plausible concept of justice? Exactly the same stricture applies to the more familiar rules of justice described in the spontaneous order theory of justice in the tradition from Hume through to Hayek and Sugden. While these rules guarantee order and predictability they are not specifically about ethically decisive entitlements to property.

In Western thought, social justice theories have filled this apparent gap. Rawls[1] and Dworkin have challenged any conception of justice that allocates property titles blindly and which uncritically permits an individualistic exploitation of natural talents. In fact, it is fairly easy to show that the Rawlsian procedure is irredeemably flawed, and not merely on utilitarian grounds. Rawls's claim that individuals' natural talents constitute a common pool to be used on behalf of the least-advantaged has counter-intuitive, even bizarre implications. It clearly implies a most peculiar notion of the self and his or her moral properties. If all extraneous features, such as natural talents and inclinations, are stripped away on the ground that they are the arbitrary results of a random nature, then what is left of the person? How do we attribute moral praise or blame when all we have left is an empty shell (Nozick, 1974, pp. 183–231), drained of those features that make a description of personhood meaningful? Indeed, it is rather paradoxical that Rawls (1971, p. 27) should stress the 'separateness of persons', in his surely correct criticism of utilitarianism that it conflates individual values into a single social maximand, when his procedure itself leaves us with no genuine human beings to separate. As has often been pointed out, there is no reason in Rawls's theory why body parts should not be redistributed on grounds of justice.

From a purely economic point of view the theory is even more defective. Despite what Rawls often says about those inequalities that are justifiable in order to generate a surplus which can be distributed to the least-advantaged, there are really no incentives for entrepreneurship to operate. Yet without it there can be no capitalism. That requires profit, but since individuals are not entitled to a return on their entrepreneurial talents they are unlikely to be motivated. Apparently, they do not own these talents. In fact, the model is a version of equilibrium or market socialism in which each factor of production is paid just enough to keep it at maximum efficiency. Rawls admits as much with his claim (1971, p. 146) that his system is indifferent between capitalist ownership or socialist ownership. However, payment to entrepreneurship (which does not have a supply price) is not rent but a reward for discovery (Kirzner, 1989). It would not exist without human action so that it is impossible to imagine some mechanical substitute for it. For that reason alone we cannot be indifferent between capitalism and socialism, even if justice required a redistribution to the least-advantaged. Indeed, in Rawls's system moral hazard would be a serious problem; everybody would have an incentive to become one of the least advantaged.

I do not suggest that the classical liberal lacuna in the moral theory of justice means that some kind of Rawlsian theory becomes irresistible. The above individualist critique would be sufficient to condemn it on efficiency grounds. However, as long as property rights and ownership are ill-defined, the theory is vulnerable to those sorts of redistributive claims that cling, however precariously, to a substantive redistributive ethic supplemented by a rational choice and quasi-efficiency based explanatory model, however implausible that is. What classical liberal theories of justice have to show is not merely that the rules recommended are serviceable in the sense of guaranteeing predictability, order and efficiency but that they also establish *just* entitlements. Entrepreneurship must be shown to be not merely a mechanism for co-ordination but also the source of justice in property holdings. Only then can co-ordination rules become proper rules of justice.

The search for such a foundation has a long history in classical liberal thought. The origins perhaps lie in Locke's moral theory of accumulation by the application of labour to previously unowned objects, subject to certain provisos. In his words, 'every Man has a Property in his own Person... The Labour of his Body, and the Work of his hands, we may say are properly his. Whatsoever then he removes out of the state that nature hath provided, and Left it in, he hath mixed his Labor with, and joyned to it something that is his own, and thereby makes it his Property' (Locke, 1960, pp. 287–8). Although this formulation has provoked tremendous controversy (Hume wondered why mixing labour should, independently of a given set of rules, establish title) it has to a great extent been the starting point for exclusively moral theories of property accumulation. This is so because it provides an individualistic challenge to rules that might locate ownership rights to privileged bodies, such as the state. It might not seem to have much application to the contemporary world since what Locke was mainly talking about, land, has been unavailable for individual appropriation for a very long time. Still, property is being created all the time in other forms, where a version of Locke's rationale might very well have a place. Finally, Locke's provisos, especially the requirement that after an appropriation there should 'be enough, and as good left' for others (1960, p. 291), have been so interpreted that there would hardly be any scope for accumulation. However, appropriate constraints have been constructed which leave the basic Lockeian liberty to accumulate intact (Nozick, 1974, pp. 178–82).

The real difficulty in reconciling abstract moral theories of justice like Locke's with the results of a certain kind of Humeian spontaneity or a Buchanan-type contracting lies in the claims to rightful possession, and property rights in general, rather than in the rules governing, say, punishment and the rectification of past wrongful acts. Those features of the backward-looking elements of justice are not likely to arouse too much controversy because they seem to be parts of the generic aspect of morality; that element which, despite the claims of relativists, seems to secure almost universal support. When it comes to ownership and entitlement to goods and property, however, the rules are subject to immense cultural variation and the views of political philosophers constitute no consensus. Adam Smith pointed to the universal propensity to 'truck, barter and exchange one thing for another' (Smith, 1976b, p. 25) but he gave little guidance as to the moral entitlement of individuals to the things that were to be traded. An exchange process must, as a matter of logic, begin with things that do not emerge from exchange, and it is the rightful possession of these that is disputed as well as the entitlements that flow from them.

Locke's labour entitlement theory has the obvious disadvantage in that it implies, as socialists have noticed, that only a certain type of meritorious or desert-based activity is worthy of reward. Yet, of course, as Hayek stressed, merit is only a contingent feature of gain in a market economy. Since a market rewards according to value it is quite likely that many valued activities display little or no merit. Indeed, what might be thought of by some critics as sheer luck plays a great role in the reward structure of capitalism. Still, one cannot deny that Locke's account of first possession (of previously unowned objects), as constitutive of original entitlement, is morally significant even though it is obvious that property is created in many other ways in complex modern economies.

The way in which we can justify ownership is to look at the process by which the market system itself works. It may or may not be the case that spontaneously developing rules will accord with a theory of just rules that derives from a more abstract and purely moral justification but it is possible that in the absence of state intervention such a convergence might eventually develop. The market has to be seen as a creative process in which human action is vital: this analysis does not merely point to its efficiency properties but also to the rightful claims that the creators have to their rewards, however arbitrary they might *appear*. If it can be shown that success in the market is not the consequence of luck, then we can meaningfully use expressions such as 'deserved' in relation to reward, even though desert here may not be harmonious with the conception used by egalitarian critics of the market. Israel Kirzner (1989) has been foremost in the attempts to construct a moral theory of reward in the market.

In his theory of entrepreneurship Kirzner, building on the insights of Mises and Hayek, shows that the market is in more or less permanent disequilibrium. This means that there are always gaps to close, differences between factor prices and anticipated product prices to exploit and opportunities for creativity in the co-ordination of knowledge. Value created in this way is qualitatively different from that which is conventionally attributed to the factors of production. It is not a result of some predictable, mechanical process but is entirely a product of mental alertness to opportunities and it is rewarded not with income as such but with profit. Significantly, profit is closely related to the correction of error in a given allocation of resources. Error correction is essential precisely because real-world economies are characterized by radical uncertainty. The moral justification for this has always been difficult for orthodox neoclassical economics since that deals only with factor earnings in equilibrium: that is much easier to justify in conventional moral terms. But the concept of pure profit is, theoretically, alien to neoclassical writers: in fact, to some it is a sign of inefficiency, if not downright immorality.

The specifically moral feature of Kirzner's explanation derives from the importance he attaches to discovery in the creation of new value:

'the entrepreneurial decision to produce, is a genuine discovery; the act that implements this discovery is an act of creation. The output that the entrepreneur produces as a result of these creative acts is thus discovered output' (Kirzner, 1989, p. 13). What this means is that value-creation depends exclusively on individual insight into the uses to which resources can be put and, since it is the product of mental awareness, it does not theoretically depend on resource ownership (capital can always be borrowed). When it is said that the entrepreneurship creates something out of nothing it is meant that a thing does not have value until someone notices, or anticipates, that it will eventually command a price. In a world of uncertainty one can never know in advance what will turn out to have value.

This has a serious implication for theories of social justice because they almost always assume a given set of resources, costlessly produced and owned by no one, which can be distributed by principles which have little to do with value-creation. This applies just as much to human resources (talents) as it does to physical ones. Dworkin (1981) tries to make a distinction between natural talents, the earnings of which no one is entitled to, and the products of efforts, and ambitions, which are fully deserved. He does this to avoid the implication in Rawls that no one properly deserves anything. But there really is no distinction, for the value of those talents can only be known through efforts and ambitions. There is no value apart from that created by ambition and effort even though the skill of the entrepreneur may not always resemble what is conventionally understood as desert-worthy activity. There is no rental income here, but only the rewards that go to those who strive to create value (fortuitous though that may sometimes look).

Kirzner's argument is a subtle variant on the Lockeian thesis; the person who discovers something is morally entitled to it because it would not exist without his or her activity. No one else owns it. What we think of as valuable natural resources, e.g. oil, do not properly exist as such until someone correctly anticipates that they will have market value. Kirzner believes that it accords with our moral intuitions because it is an exemplification of the 'finders-keepers' rule. This is indeed a not uncommon ethical practice: we do regard the discoverer of something, especially a scientific or medical innovation, as being entitled to its rewards. However, Kirzner's theory would apply to much more controversial areas. For example, the corporate raider who notices that certain assets are undervalued on the stock market, buys them up with borrowed money and organizes them in profitable ways, no doubt creates new value but one questions whether his activity is worthy of the same moral approbation as that of a person who profits from the discovery of a cure for a serious disease. Conventional morality does not regard the two types of discovery as morally similar, especially as the raider is often accused of causing unemployment.

Regardless of this point, which reflects a common moral prejudice that yearns for objective measures of value, there are further difficulties in the application of the finders-keepers principle. Does it not rest on the exploitation of people's ignorance? Can a distinction be drawn between genuine discovery and fraud? The second point is perhaps ethically more serious since there may be well-founded doubts about ownership: especially in stock market transactions (Barry, 1991, chapter 3) where information is at a premium. On the assumption that entrepreneurship takes place within the firm it is quite unclear whether employees, who actually make discoveries, are entitled to all the rewards (perhaps by trading on undisclosed information on the stock market) or whether the owners are. Even Kirzner (1989, pp. 172–3) admits that there may be doubts concerning ownership, about what the act of discovery actually consists of. Particular circumstances may make it impossible to apply directly the finders-keepers principle. We apparently have to rely on tradition and conventional legal interpretations with regard to ownership. Attention to these practices may, however, involve a dilution of the principle.

This point brings us back to the original problem: the connection between rules of justice derived from convention and those (like Kirzner's) that emanate from more abstract and universal notions of morality. A classical liberal theory of justice runs into difficulties when these two approaches collide, as potentially they can. Direct and uncontroversial applications of finders-keepers may be rarer than Kirzner supposes. It is quite likely that conventions, which may not always accord with the abstract morality of individualism, will, nevertheless, have a greater claim on people's intuitions as they gradually become internalized in a Humeian manner.

In certain cases, communal rights of ownership (especially of scarce natural resources, such as water) may develop which will put strict limits on the possibilities of discovery alone creating private property rights. There is nothing to stop the determined classical liberal theorists of justice maintaining that ownership must always inhere in individuals, and that this is validated by a rationalistic natural law, despite what convention might imply. However, this rationalistic approach may not always cohere with our moral intuitions, which are often inspired by a broader conception of desert than that permitted by classical liberalism. Still, such an approach provides a much-needed supplement to a Hayekian theory which is curiously silent on those distributive problems and disputes about ownership that are not catered for by pure procedural rules. Something like Kirzner's theory is required if the traditional Lockeian justification for ownership is to be given a modern application and the morality of capitalism demonstrated.

Note

1. Rawls (1993) has altered the theoretical foundations of his theory of social justice but its egalitarian thrust remains the same.

13. Classical Liberalism and Civil Society

It might have been thought that, with the spread of market capitalism and the growing distaste for the state, classical liberalism would have experienced something of an intellectual renaissance. It is clear that this is not taking place. Various forms of interventionism still retain their grip on the imagination of social theorists and political philosophers. The intellectual debate has certainly shifted from arguments between proponents of capitalism and advocates of central planning to issues about the different types of market capitalism, but the distinctive features of classical liberalism have become somewhat blurred in this intellectual reorientation. It is even said that the doctrine only had relevance to the historic battle against Marxism: and now that the latter has little relevance to the modern world the central tenets of individualism are likewise of limited application.

One reason for this might be the fact that, as mentioned earlier, classical liberalism has certain ideological overtones. To some extent it presents itself as a doctrine of universal applicability and for that reason seems to be incapable of accounting for the nuances of the differing social and economic forms that might be encompassed under the broad heading of market capitalism. Evidence of this is readily apparent in the varieties of corporate organization that are revealed by the most cursory examination of existing market societies. The Anglo-American style of business, with its 'loosely-held' form of corporate government in which anonymous shareholders, concerned only with immediate gratification, drive the economy, is often contrasted unfavourably with the more intimate style of corporate organization practiced, say, in Germany (Barry, 1993a), where owners are more closely linked with management and apparently concerned with the social effects of business activity.

This has not only efficiency implications (indeed it is a fundamental claim of classical liberal epistemics that it is impossible to know a priori which type of economic management will be successful) but also moral ones. For Anglo-American capitalism has come under increasing critical fire precisely because of its anonymity; its alleged Mandevillian, amoral motivations are said to be corrosive of those communal bonds that are thought to be essential for the maintenance of civility. If classical liberalism does embody these features (which may be doubted) it is thought to be irrelevant for communities whose history and traditions make them quite unsuitable for an easy transplant of individualism. It is to some extent true that classical liberals have presented a vision of the good society as one in which anonymous agents are held together by very general rules and these individuals tend to be identified independently of discrete communal affiliations. It is also the case that some writers have naïvely held that spontaneous processes and competition between rival political and social forms would somehow lead to the triumph of specifically liberal orders, characterized in the above way.

Against the ambitious geopolitical claims of some, but by no means all, classical liberals a rival theory has emerged in recent decades: the idea of 'civil society' (Gray, 1993, pp. 283–328). Although many of the features of individualism are embedded in this doctrine, significant departures have been made from it to justify the claim that civil society represents a new and superior normative goal. It is true that some of the dissenters in Eastern Europe used the idea, in their struggle against communism, as representative of something different from Western liberalism, and more akin to a European tradition of civility that had been obliterated by communism.

Civil society recognizes an essential pluralism in human values, that there is no one way of life that has a unique hold on our reason and that the good society cannot be identified with an unsullied individualism or collectivism. Differing forms of social organization can coexist under the rule of law as long as the state is precluded from exclusive control of all aspects of life. The state is viewed, almost in a Hegelian manner, as a kind of neutral arbiter of disputes, an impartial guarantor of stability charged with the responsibility of preventing one subset of society predominating over all others. Of course, in an obvious tribute to classical liberal jurisprudence, theorists of civil society insist that the state itself should be bound by law, as in the idea of the *Rechtsstaat*.

Furthermore, civil society does not accept that the relentless operation of market forces alone is sufficient to meet with the idea of order and humanity. That is why in the theory of the social market economy the state was given the responsibility of preventing an unaided market disintegrating into monopolies and cartels and therefore spontaneously destroying the order of freedom. Though it should be pointed out here (Tumlir, 1989) that some writers in the tradition held that a strengthened civil law was a more effective device for maintaining market freedom than was the state.

Again, theorists of civil society are not against the state having a welfare role (though it is vastly different from that in Western democracies). It is mandated not merely by a morality of benevolence but also by the desire to preserve a special kind of ordered liberty: the victims of relentless market process are not merely in need in a tangible sense but they are also disabled from participation in civil society as full citizens. A theory of citizenship is now being developed which maintains that capitalism is unstable if it fails to integrate everyone fully into its economic and social structure.

One is entitled to ask whether all this represents a radical departure from classical liberalism. Of course, the slightly more benign attitude towards the state that civil-society theory evinces is vulnerable to the severe criticism of public-choice theory. This has successfully demonstrated that its officials in a democracy can be as predatory as any market trader driven by self-interest. But the idea of proper constitutionalism is common to both doctrines, though the excessive legalism of anonymous market orders has led theorists of civil society to favour more communal modes of dispute-settling and less individualistic types of adjustment to change. If classical liberalism is presented as an ideology, whose features never change and which is appropriate to all social circumstances, then the theorists of civil society would undoubtedly have a point. But this is a caricature of the doctrine.

Classical liberalism is not an ideology in this crude sense. Since its central tenet is liberty the doctrine necessarily allows for differing forms of social organization, operating within the rule of law, to develop. Its stress on voluntarism means that communal and non-market associations, e.g. churches, welfare associations and private educational foundations, can flourish under the aegis of common rules of just conduct. If anything, liberal egalitarianism, with its goal of shifting the social order towards an end-state of substantive equality, is far more ideological. The existence of classical liberal orders, however imperfect, and forms of civil society, is in fact a threat to liberal egalitarianism. This is because the pluralism they encourage and the variety of institutional arrangements they generate constitute potential sources of inequality which the liberal egalitarian will want to eliminate by use of the state's power. Although theorists of civil society have a more favourable attitude to the welfare state than do classical liberals they are hostile to the kind of welfarism that has developed in contemporary social democracies.

Classical liberal theories of procedural justice are necessary, if not quite sufficient, for the preservation of most of the values of civil society. The main features of this order are surely reproducible without the help of social justice. That may be a type of universalism but it is certainly a very modest one. If there are generic moral principles for mankind, as most people would agree, then classical liberalism has contributed much to their articulation, both practically and philosophically. This holds true independently of the obvious discoveries that the doctrine has made in economic theory and organization.

References

Axelrod, R. (1984), *The Evolution of Co-operation*, New York: Basic Books.

Barry, B. (1965), *Political Argument*, London: Routledge and Kegan Paul.

Barry, N.P. (1984), 'Ideas Versus Interests: The Classical Liberal Dilemma', in N. P. Barry, *et al.*, *Hayek's 'Serfdom' Revisited*, London: Institute of Economic Affairs.

Barry, N.P. (1986), *On Classical Liberalism and Libertarianism*, London: Macmillan.

Barry, N.P. (1989), 'Ideas and Interests: The Problem Reconsidered', in A. Gamble, *et al.*, *Ideas, Interests and Consequences*, London: Institute of Economic Affairs.

Barry, N.P. (1991), *The Morality of Business Enterprise*, Aberdeen: Aberdeen University Press.

Barry, N.P. (1993a), 'The Social Market Economy', *Social Philosophy and Policy*, **10**, 1–25.

Barry, N.P. (1993b), 'Sovereignty, the Rule of Recognition and Constitutional Stability in Britain', *Journal des Economistes et des Etudes Humaines*, **4**, 159–76.

Benson, B. (1990), *The Enterprise of Law*, San Francisco: Pacific Research Institute for Public Policy.

Berlin, I. (1958), *Two Concepts of Liberty*, London: Oxford University Press.

Böhm, F. (1960), *Reden und Schriften*, Karlsruhe: C.F. Müller.

Böhm, F. (1989), 'The Rule of Law', in A. Peacock and H. Willgerodt (eds), *Germany's Social Market Economy*, London: Macmillan.

Buchanan, J.M. (1975), *The Limits of Liberty. Between Anarchy and Leviathan*, Chicago: University of Chicago Press.

Buchanan, J.M. (1977), *Freedom in Constitutional Contract*, Austin, Texas: A. & M. University Press.

Buchanan, J.M. and Tullock, G. (1962), *The Calculus of Consent*, Ann Arbor: University of Michigan Press.

Coase, R.H. (1960), 'The Problem of Social Cost', *Journal of Law and Economics*, **3**, 1–44.

Cohen, G. (1979), 'Capitalism, Freedom and the Proletariat', in A. Ryan (ed.), *The Idea of Freedom*, Oxford: Clarendon Press.

De Jasay, A. (1985), *The State*, Oxford: Basil Blackwell.

De Jasay, A. (1991), *Choice, Contract, Consent*, London: Institute of Economic Affairs.

Dicey, A.V. (1926), *Law and Opinion in England*, 2nd ed., London: Macmillan.

Dworkin, R. (1977), *Taking Rights Seriously*, London: Duckworth.

Dworkin, R. (1981), 'Equality of Resources', *Philosophy and Public Affairs*, **10**, 283–345.

Dworkin, R. (1985), *A Matter of Principle*, Cambridge: Harvard University Press.

Dworkin, R. (1986), *Law's Empire*, London: Fontana.

Epstein, R.A. (1985), *Takings: Private Property and the Power of Eminent Domain*, Cambridge: Harvard University Press.

Eucken, W. (1950), *The Foundations of Economics*, Edinburgh: William Hodge.

Eucken, W. (1951), *This Unsuccessful Age*, Edinburgh: William Hodge.

Giersch, H., Paque, K. and Schmieding, H. (1992), *The Fading Miracle*, Cambridge: Cambridge University Press.

Gray, J. (1989), *Liberalisms: Essays in Political Philosophy*, London: Routledge.

Gray, J. (1992), *The Moral Foundations of Market Institutions*, London: Institute of Economic Affairs.

Gray, J. (1993), *Post-Liberalism: Studies in Political Thought*, London: Routledge.

Green, T.H. (1888), *Works*, edited by R. Nettleship, London: Oxford University Press.

Hamm, W. (1989), 'The Welfare State at its Limit', in A. Peacock and H. Willgerodt, *Germany Neo-Liberals and the Social Market Economy*, London: Macmillan.

Hart, H.L.A. (1961), *The Concept of Law*, London: Oxford University Press.

Hayek, F.A. (1948), *Individualism and Economic Order*, London: Routledge and Kegan Paul.

Hayek, F.A. (1960), *The Constitution of Liberty*, London: Routledge and Kegan Paul.

Hayek, F.A. (1967), *Studies in Philosophy, Politics and Economics*, London: Routledge and Kegan Paul.

Hayek, F.A. (1973), *Rules and Order*, London: Routledge and Kegan Paul.

Hayek, F.A. (1976), *The Mirage of Social Justice*, London: Routledge and Kegan Paul.

Hayek, F.A. (1978), *The Denationalisation of Money*, 2nd edition, London: Institute of Economic Affairs.

Hayek, F.A. (1979), *The Political Order of a Free People*, London: Routledge and Kegan Paul.

Hayek, F.A. (1988), *The Fatal Conceit*, London: Routledge.

Hume, D. (1953), *Hume's Political Essays*, edited by C. Hendel, New York: Liberal Arts Press. Originally published 1748.

Hume, D. (1972), *A Treatise of Human Nature*, London: Fontana. Originally published 1739.

Kirzner, I. (1973), *Competition and Entrepreneurship*, Chicago: University of Chicago Press.

Kirzner, I. (1979), *Perception, Opportunity and Profit*, Chicago: University of Chicago Press.

Kirzner, I. (1989), *Discovery, Capitalism and Distributive Justice*, Oxford: Basil Blackwell.

Kukathas, C. (1992), 'Freedom versus Autonomy', in J. Gray, *The Moral Foundations of Market Institutions*, London: Institute of Economic Affairs.

Le Grand, J. (1982), *The Strategy of Equality*, London: Allen and Unwin.

Lenel, H. (1989), 'Evolution of the Social Market Economy', in A. Peacock and H. Willgerodt, *German Neo-Liberals and the Social Market Economy*, London: Macmillan.

Locke, J. (1960), *Two Treatises of Government*, edited by P. Laslett, Cambridge: Cambridge University Press. Originally published in 1690.

MacIntyre, A. (1981), *After Virtue*, London: Duckworth.

Maine, H. (1885), *Popular Government*, London: John Murray.

Mandeville, B. (1924), *The Fable of the Bees*, edited by F.B. Kaye, London: Oxford University Press. Originally published 1705.

Manne, H. (21965), 'Mergers and the Market for Corporate Control', *Journal of Political Economy*, **73**, 110–20.

Mills, J.S. (1848), *Principles of Political Economy*, London: J.W. Parker.

Mises, L. (1949), *Human Action*, Chicago: Henry Regnery.

Mises, L. (1962), *Liberalism*, Kansas: Sheed, Andrews and McMeel.

Mulhall, S. and Swift, A. (1992), *Liberals and Communitarians*, Oxford: Basil Blackwell.

Müller-Armack, A. (1965), 'The Principles of the Social Market Economy', *German Economic Review*, **3**, 80–96.

Müller-Armack, A. (1979), 'Economic Systems from a Social Point of View', in J. Thesing (ed.), *Economy and Development*, Mainz: Konrad Adenauer-Stiftung.

Nozick, R. (1974), *Anarchy, State and Utopia*, New York: Basic Books.

Nozick, R. (1990), *The Examined Life: Philosophical Meditations*, New York: Simon and Schuster.

Plant, R. (1991), *Modern Political Thought*, Oxford: Basil Blackwell.

Popper, K. (1957), *The Poverty of Historicism*, London: Routledge and Kegan Paul.

Rawls, J. (1971), *A Theory of Justice*, Cambridge: Harvard University Press.

Rawls, J. (1993), *Political Liberalism*, New York: Columbia University Press.

Raz, J. (1986), *The Morality of Freedom*, London: Oxford University Press.

Robbins, L. (1935), *The Nature and Significance of Economic Science*, 2nd edition, London: Routledge and Kegan Paul.

Röpke, W. (1950), *The Social Crisis of Our Time*, Edinburgh: William Hodge.

Röpke, W. (1960), *A Humane Economy*, London: Wolf.

Sandel, M. (1982), *Liberalism and the Limits of Justice*, Cambridge: Cambridge University Press.

Siegan, B. (1980), *Economic Liberties and the Constitution*, Chicago: University of Chicago Press.

Smith, A. (1969), *The Theory of Moral Sentiments*, edited by E. West, Indianapolis: Liberty Press. Originally published 1759.

Smith, A. (1976a), *The Theory of Moral Sentiments*, edited by D.D. Raphael and A.L. Macfie, Oxford: Clarendon Press. Originally published 1759.

Smith, A. (1976b), *An Enquiry into the Nature and Causes of the Wealth of Nations*, edited by R.H. Campbell and A.S. Skinner, Oxford: Clarendon Press. Originally published 1776.

Steiner, A. (1974), 'Individual Liberty', *Proceedings of the Aristotelian Society*, Oxford: Basil Blackwell.

Sugden, R. (1986), *The Economics of Rights, Co-operation and Welfare*, Oxford: Basil Blackwell.

Taylor, C. (1985), *Philosophical Papers*, Cambridge: Cambridge University Press.

Tiebout, C. (1956, 'A Pure Theory of Local Expenditure', *Journal of Political Economy*, **64**, 416–24.

Trakman, L. (1983), *The Law Merchant*, Littleton: Rothman.

Tullock, G. (1976), *The Vote Motive*, London: Institute of Economic Affairs.

Tumlir, J. (1989), 'Franz Böhm and the Development of Economic-Constitutional Analysis', in A. Peacock and H. Willgerodt, *German Neo-Liberals and the Social Market Economy*, London: Macmillan.

Wagner, R. (1993), 'Parchment, Guns and Constitutional Order', in C. Rowley, (ed.), *Property Rights and the Limits of Democracy*, Aldershot: Edward Elgar, for the Locke Institute.

Wallich, H. (1955), *Mainsprings of the German Revival*, New Haven: Yale University Press.

Walzer, M. (1983), *Spheres of Justice*, New York: Basic Books.

Index

accumulation, theory of 64–5
affirmative action 31
agreement
    and social institutions 55
    truth and 54
Albania: freedom in 46–7
Anglo-American capitalism 70–71
authoritarianism and liberty 44
autonomy
    and liberty 47–52
    opportunity costs of 50
    and taxation 50
Axelrod, R. 19

Barry, N.P. 21, 26, 39, 41, 44, 56, 68,
    70
Benson, B. 18
Bentham, J. 40
Böhm, F. 21–2
Buchanan, James 3, 8, 27, 63
    on contractarian liberty 54, 55,
        56–7

cartelization, in Germany 22
choice
    and liberty 46, 48
    and moral evaluation 53, 55
    and social institutions 55
civil liberties 31, 33–4
civil society 70–73
    and market forces 71–2
    pluralism in 71
classical liberalism
    and civil society 70–73
    and communitarianism 2–3
    constitutional failure to protect 25,
        30
    current state of 1–4
    and egalitarianism 3–4, 28, 31

as ideology 5–7, 26
individualism of 6–7
institutional framework of 3
interests theory of 26–7
and judiciary 35–6
and justice 58–69
    and entrepreneurship 64–5
    problems 62–3
legalism in 36
limited scope of 6
morality in 9–10
realism of 8–10
scientific component of 5–6
Coase, R. 29
coercion 47
Cohen, G. 44–5
collectivism
    in Great Britain 38
    and restriction 45
common forms of life 51
common law 26
    and judiciary 28–31, 33
    and market system 28
    spontaneous order theory in 27–8
communism 14
communitarianism and classical
    liberalism 2–3, 35
competition and government choice
    41
constitutionalism 5
    and classical liberalism 1
    and morality 56–7
    and sovereignty 37–9
contractarian liberty 53–7
contracts
    freedom in 21
    and law 28
    and markets 17–18
    in protective state 54–5

6-80   *Classical Liberalism in the Age of Post-Communism*

restrictions on 26, 31, 34
cooperation in markets 18–19
co-ordination games 19
Council of Ministers (European
    Community) 42
creativity and markets 16

de Jasay, Anthony 1, 25
democracy 25
    and liberty 40–42
Dicey, A.V. 26
division of labour 17
Dworkin, R. 26, 31, 32, 33, 34, 35
    on justice 58, 59, 63, 67

economic liberty 33–4
entrepreneurship 16
    and classical liberalism 64–5
    and discovery 68
    and justice 62–3
    and ownership 66–7
Epstein, R.A. 31
equality
    moral and economic 58–9
    and ownership 59
Eucken, W. 21
European Community 41–2
European Court of Justice 42
evaluation in markets 53

fairness 54
federalism 41–2
'finders-keepers' rule 67–8
free rider problem 18
freedom 2
    and choice 46, 53
    of contract 21
    and *Ordo* liberalism (Germany) 21
    and resources 48

*Garcia v. San Antonio Transit
    Authority* 41
German market economy 20–24
Giersch, H. 23
government
    and competition 41
    constraints on
        in classical liberalism 9

by rights 33
as entity 25
limited in classical liberalism 5
and self-interest 13
subjected to rule of law 37–8
Gray, J. 2, 23, 53, 71
    on liberty 47, 48, 49, 51
    on markets 14–15, 17
Great Britain
    collectivism in 38
    constitutionalism in 38–9
    parliament, sovereignty of 39
Green, T.H. 26

Hamm, W. 21
Hart, H.L.A. 39
Hayek, F.A. 3–4, 11, 13, 16, 18, 22,
    38
    on constitution 26, 28–36
    on justice 61, 62, 65
    on liberty 41, 42
Hobbes, Thomas 12, 18, 55
human wants 8
Hume, David 8, 9, 11, 12, 13, 14, 17,
    35, 43

income distribution, and justice 61
individual, abstract 2–3
individualism of classical liberalism
    6–7
inequality and justice 63–4
information
    lack of 8
    in markets 15–16
inheritance 59
institutional framework in classical
    liberalism 3

judiciary
    changes in 34–5
    and classical liberalism 34–5
    and common law 28–31
    discovering law 32
    and liberal egalitarianism 33
    rights, protecting 32–3
justice 1, 14, 16, 58–69
    backward-looking 60
    in classical liberalism 60